THE VISUAL DIRECTORY OF
BIRDS
OF NORTH AMERICA

Quarto

© 2025 Quarto Publishing Group USA Inc.

This edition published in 2025 by Chartwell Books,
an imprint of The Quarto Group
142 West 36th Street, 4th Floor
New York, NY 10018 USA
T (212) 779-4972
www.Quarto.com

Contains content originally published as *A Field Guide to Backyard Birds of North America*
(2023), *A Field Guide to Songbirds of North America* (2021), and *1000 Birds* (2017) by
Chartwell Books, an imprint of The Quarto Group, 142 West 36th Street, 4th Floor, New York,
NY 10018 USA.

10 9 8 7 6 5 4 3 2 1

Chartwell titles are also available at discount for retail, wholesale, promotional, and bulk
purchase. For details, contact the Special Sales Manager by email at specialsales@quarto.
com or by mail at The Quarto Group, Attn: Special Sales Manager, 100 Cummings Center
Suite 265D, Beverly, MA 01915, USA.

ISBN: 978-0-7858-4733-5

Publisher: Wendy Friedman
Publishing Director: Meredith Mennitt
Designer: Angelika Piwowarczyk

Printed in China

EEA Representation, WTS Tax d.o.o.,
Žanova ulica 3, 4000 Kranj, Slovenia.
www.wts-tax.si

*A Field Guide to Backyard Birds of
North America:*

Assistant Editor: Charlene
Fernandes
Editorial Assistant: Ella Whiting
Junior Designer: India Minter
Designer: Sally Bond
Art Director: Gemma Wilson
Sales Director: Nikki Tilbury
Publisher: Lorraine Dickey

*A Field Guide to Songbirds of North
America:*

Project editor: Liz Pasfield
Art editor/Designer: Tania Field
Assistant art director: Penny Cobb
Copy editor: Claire Waite Brown
Bird artist: David Ord Kerr
Illustrators: Vana Haggerty and
Wayne Ford
Picture researcher: Claudia Tate
Art director: Moira Clinch
Publisher: Samantha Warrington

THE VISUAL DIRECTORY OF
BIRDS
OF NORTH AMERICA

DISCOVERING THE CONTINENT'S
MOST CAPTIVATING BIRDS

chartwell
books

TABLE OF CONTENTS

INTRODUCTION

What is it that draws us to birds? Why is it that watching birds is one of the fastest growing hobbies in the world? There is no single answer, but rather a multitude of answers that are all focused on the bird-human interface: most birds are active when we are active.

Their language to us is the language of music—song, percussion, rhythmic, soothing, excited, incredibly varied, yet predictable so that we can identify birds by their voices as we would identify an old friend on the telephone. Birds are often colorful, with each species sporting unique hues and patterns of plumage that allow us to identify it as we might recognize an acquaintance on a busy street.

Our fine-feathered friends

Birds remind us of family and friends by behaviors ranging from the protective attention of parent birds toward their young, to the rambunctious "Feed me! Feed me!" demands of a fledgling, to the bill held high in a face-off of two birds in a territorial dispute at a mutual boundary, to the intimate collaboration of a pair constructing a nest, to the perceived joy in the songs of birds proclaiming the arrival

of spring and the beginning of a new cycle of life. In short we are drawn to birds by their "human" qualities—which, of course, are not human at all, but the perception of our inquisitive minds.

Perhaps we are drawn to birds out of envy— that ability to fly, to soar above the clouds? Or perhaps it is merely the wonder we feel on observing the aerobatics of swallows, the speed of falcons, the effortless soaring of an eagle, the precision flight of a skein of geese or a wheeling flock of hundreds of blackbirds that seems to pulse as if the flock itself were a living being.

We are also drawn to birds by hope. Perhaps it is the hope that they might take advantage of the well-stocked feeder or birdbath we so carefully selected and placed in the garden. Maybe it is the dream that a new species will appear in our yard or that we might find a particular rare bird on a trip to its reported

MALLARDS
These ducks rarely dive into the water for food, preferring to grab morsels on the water's surface.

haunts. Or maybe it is the hope we have with the warming days of spring that the birds that nested nearby last year will return.

Perhaps it is the sense of satisfaction, pride, fulfillment, and maybe even the power that we might feel when bluebirds take up residence in the birdhouse we just built and carefully located in our backyard. Perhaps it is our amazement at their arrival back in our yards after hard winters and long migrations. How could we not respect these tiny feathered creatures that dauntlessly withstand snow and storms, heat and drought, and then saucily proclaim their survival with beautiful song. Perhaps it is seeing the awe on a child's face when peering for the first time into a bird nest with eggs or nestlings.

Birds share our lives by contributing to our aesthetic senses and emotional well-being, but they are also, in a sense, our "protectors," consuming insect pests and weed seeds and serving in many ways as barometers of the health of the ecosystems in which we live. Yes, they can be a nuisance. Blackbirds and European Starlings can consume crops and sometimes monopolize our feeders, but they also consume cutworms and other harmful pests. All too often with such birds, we think only of the negative. Proper accounting demands that we look at both sides of the ledger. And we should take a closer look at the ledger of our relationships to birds. We might provide feed and shelter for birds in our yards, but how much of their habitat have we destroyed?

A new relationship

This book is a primer for understanding our relationship with birds and their relationship with us. It provides a window on the intimate lives of birds and how they cope with the world in which we both live. Paired with a field guide

GREAT SPOTTED WOODPECKER
Its "drumming," usually on dead wood, can be heard up to half a mile away.

and a pair of binoculars, this book can open your eyes to a wonderful world that has been there all along, but which so often has gone "unseen." Only once you know what you are looking at, can you experience it fully. It is the beginning of a beautiful friendship.

Use a logbook to record the comings and goings of birds. When did they arrive in spring? When did they build their nest? How many young did they raise? What were they eating? How did they interact with other birds? While we know a great deal about birds, there is much we don't know. Share your discoveries and learn from others. Get involved with a local bird club, Audubon chapter, or regional ornithological society. The wonder of birds and excitement of birding is yours for life.

Jerome A. Jackson (Professor of Biology) and Bette J. S. Jackson (Associate Professor of Biology) Florida Gulf Coast University

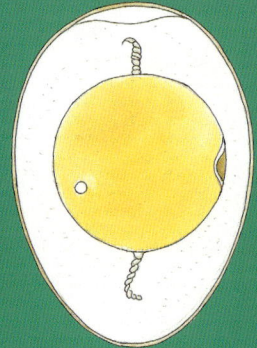

CHAPTER ONE

BIRD LIFE

This chapter reveals the incredible world of birds. The more you know about their world—their struggle for survival, migration patterns, predatory habits—the greater your involvement and enjoyment in bird-watching. Why does a warbler's bill differ so greatly from a macaw's, or the feet of a Harpy Eagle from those of a cormorant? Does plumage change with the seasons? An appreciation of bird anatomy will help you understand why a bird has a particular habitat and prey and has certain behavioral patterns.

BIRD ANATOMY

Birds exhibit a wide range of biological adaptations that distinguish them from other animals; many of these are geared toward flight, the single most distinguishing feature of birds. The anatomy of flying birds is a superb example of the compromise between structural strength and low weight that is needed to achieve efficient flight. Other adaptations help different birds survive in their particular habitat.

In common with other warm-blooded vertebrates (animals with backbones) such as mammals, birds have a rigid, bony skeleton that supports and protects the soft tissues and organs within the rib cage and provides anchorage for the muscles.

The skeleton
Bird skeletons, however, have evolved from the heavy structures of their reptilian ancestors into much lighter, but sturdier, frameworks. The larger bones of flying birds are hollow and reinforced with a network of crossbars—like the truss on a bridge, this structure combines great strength with low weight, giving the bird a low take-off weight and a high power-to-weight ratio, which is vital for efficient flight. Besides being hollow, many bird bones are fused together, which reduces flexibility, but greatly increases strength in order to resist the great forces birds experience during flight, especially during take-off and landing.

Head
A bird's head is small, with lightweight, cavity-filled skull bones, and typically very large round orbits, or eye sockets. Their toothless jaws, which are the foundation of the beak, vary greatly in shape according to the specific, often diet-related, tasks for which these tools are needed (see Birds' Bills, pp. 14–17, and Birds' Feet, pp. 18–19). The underside of the lower jaw consists of a soft throat pouch, or gular region, which is little developed in birds such as sparrows and finches, more obvious in some, such as cormorants, and most evident in the remarkable extensible pouch of the pelicans. The upper bill has openings for the nostrils, usually close to the base. The lower bill allows little or no sideways, or chewing, movement. In many birds, especially swifts, nightjars, and other insect-eaters, the bill is relatively small but the mouth, or gape, is very wide.

Spine, pelvis, and legs
The "wishbone" consists of two clavicles, or collarbones, fused together to act as a strengthening strut that braces the wings apart. Flightless birds and some others, such as the parrots, have a greatly reduced wishbone. A bird's neck varies greatly among species in length and mobility, but in all birds, the bones of the spine are mostly fused together to form a solid, rigid unit that is firmly attached to the large pelvic girdle. The pelvic bones are also fused, and act with the rigid spine to distribute the weight of the body during landing. The lightweight leg bones are operated by powerful muscles on the upper leg, but only by tendons on the lower leg—this sturdy, compact structure acts as a shock absorber during landing. Birds' feet vary greatly in size and form, playing vital roles in

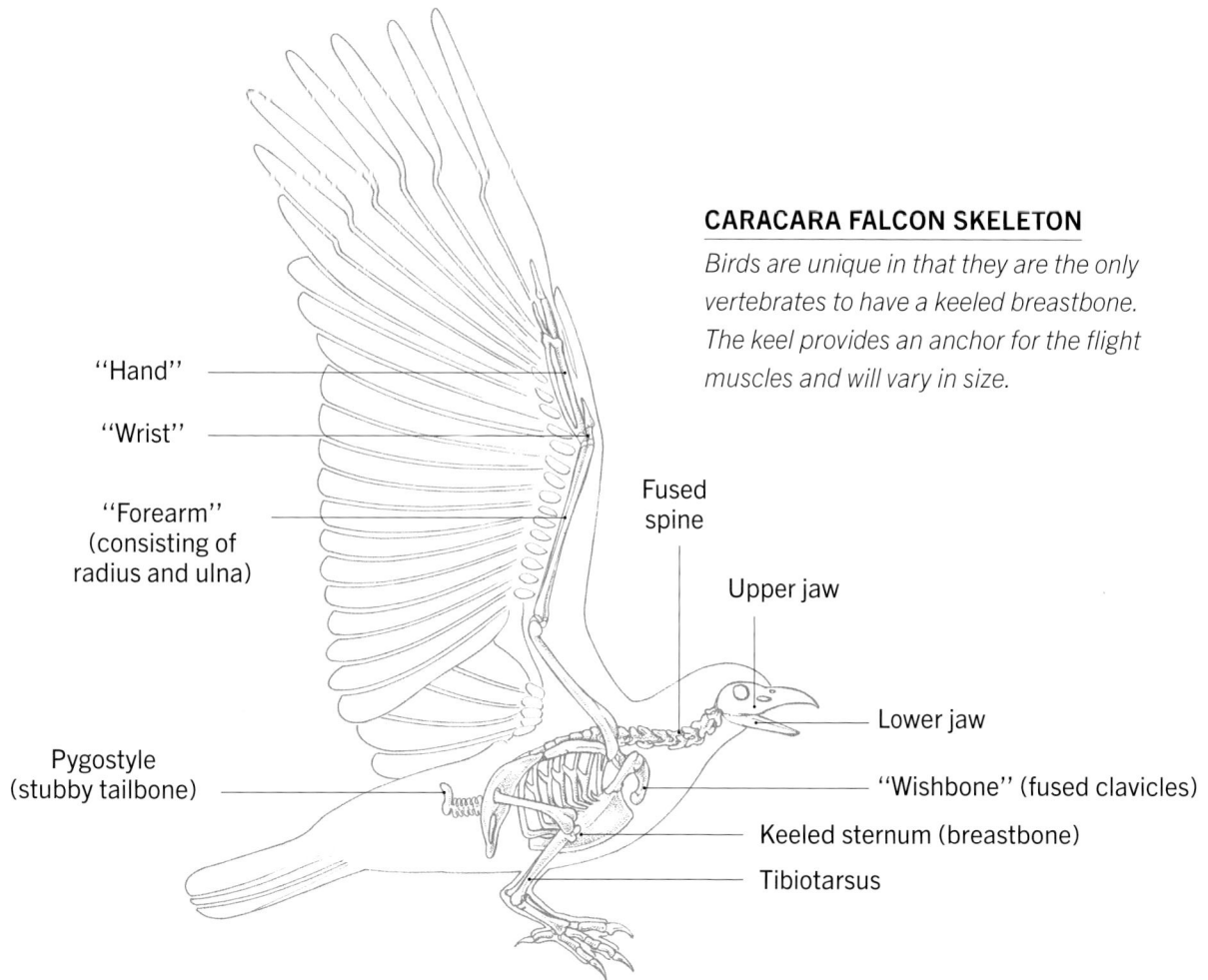

CARACARA FALCON SKELETON

Birds are unique in that they are the only vertebrates to have a keeled breastbone. The keel provides an anchor for the flight muscles and will vary in size.

"Hand"

"Wrist"

"Forearm" (consisting of radius and ulna)

Fused spine

Upper jaw

Lower jaw

Pygostyle (stubby tailbone)

"Wishbone" (fused clavicles)

Keeled sternum (breastbone)

Tibiotarsus

locomotion and feeding (see Bills and Feet, pp. 14–19).

has several fused digits but a separate thumb (see Feathers, pp. 12–13).

Breast and wings

The breastbone, or sternum, varies from family to family; in gliding birds it is smaller, but in those with powerful, deep wingbeats, such as pigeons, it is large and has a prominent ridge, or keel. The relatively massive breast muscles, or pectorals, attach to the keel, which provides a deep anchorage for the powerful downward sweep of the wings made by contracting the pectorals. The wing is reminiscent of a mammal's arm or forelimb, but with variations: the upper arm is generally embedded in the body or hidden beneath the body feathers. The "inner wing" corresponds to the human forearm (the radius and ulna) and the outer wing, beyond the "wrist," to the "hand," which

Respiratory system

Birds have developed a highly specialized respiratory and circulatory system that allow them to metabolize oxygen and other substances rapidly so that vast amounts of energy can be generated—relative to their size—to power their wings. Air first passes into the lungs, and then farther into extensions of the lungs called air sacs that reach into the bird's hollow bones, before passing out through the lungs again, allowing the bird to take oxygen on each passage. A bird's heart also beats very rapidly to move the oxygen: a hummingbird has up to 1,000 heartbeats a minute during flight.

Feathers

A feather is an amazing structure. It is made of keratin, a hornlike substance that also forms the basis of our fingernails. It is lightweight, yet strong and durable—essential structural requirements for a bird to achieve flight.

Each feather has a main shaft, or rachis, from which extends a "vane" on each side, consisting of scores of small, interlinked branches called barbs. The base of the shaft is hollow to maximize strength and minimize weight. Together, these make up the basic leaflike shape of the whole feather.

Zipped together

The barbs are held together in a complex series of indentations and hooks called barbules, which interlink in a similar way to Velcro. If the barbules become detached, the feather appears disarranged and ragged. Birds preen regularly every day, each one spending long periods of time gently but firmly sliding its feathers one by one through its bill. This action removes any

debris from the feather, zips the barbs together again, and keeps them in good shape.

Flight feathers are stiff and usually slightly curved. Smaller feathers tend to be wider, and less rigid, especially at the base, where some of the vane is composed of loose and wispy barbs. These barbs at the base of the shaft are almost entirely lacking the barbules that zip the rest of the feather together. They create a soft, down-like layer that insulates against heat and cold.

The main feather tracts

If you spread a bird's wing, you will see that the feathers are arranged in neat zones. Forming the wingtip are large, long, stiff feathers that grow from the fused "fingers" of the "hand"—these are the primary feathers and are of different lengths. Along the trailing edge of the inner half of the wing are the secondary feathers, which are also stiff but shorter than the primaries. These grow from the "forearm." Just beyond the bend of the wing is the bird's "thumb," from which grows a small tuft of feathers that can be raised from the main surface of the wing in flight. This is called the "alula," or bastard wing. The alula is important in helping a bird maneuver in the air at low speeds, and it has long been emulated in aircraft designs.

Each of the main tracts of flight feathers of the wings and tail is covered at its base by a

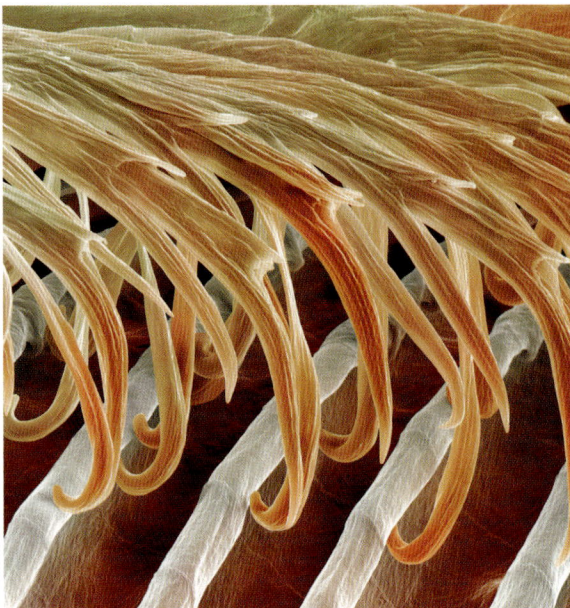

BARBULES
Feathers have a brilliant hook-fastener construction, with thousands of tiny hooks clinging to minute stays.

WING ANATOMY

The main tracts of flight feathers on a bird's wings, such as the primaries and secondaries, are overlapped by the coverts—various series of smaller feathers that merge with the main tracts to form an aerodynamic surface.

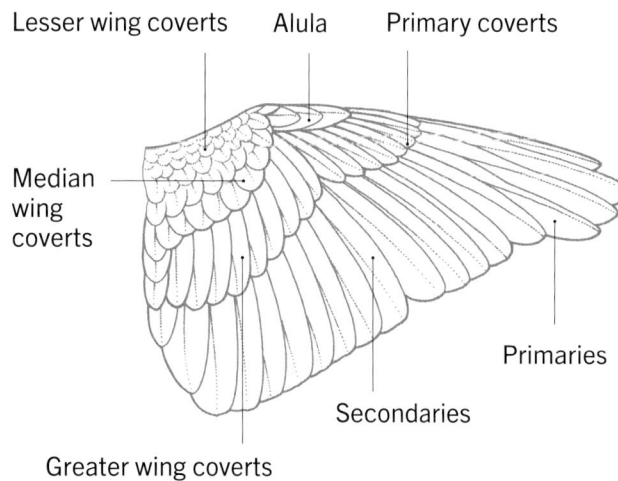

Lesser wing coverts

Alula

Primary coverts

Median wing coverts

Primaries

Secondaries

Greater wing coverts

row of smaller feathers—the coverts, which cover the gaps at the base of the flight feathers, creating a smooth, solid surface for efficient flight. The contour feathers on the bird's body are less obviously, yet still precisely, arranged, cloaking the body to give it its streamlined shape. There are areas of a bird's body that are less defined by feather tracts than by color and pattern, such as the forehead, crown, nape, cheeks, breast, and flank.

Wear and tear

Feathers gradually become ragged and lose color. The pigments that provide most of the colors in plumage (see Colors and Patterns, pp. 20–21) fade with age, especially if they are exposed to strong sun or saltwater. These exposed parts become paler and duller while the base, usually covered by other feathers, remains bright and fresh.

Molt

Feathers, once grown, are dead structures that gradually wear and deteriorate. To counteract this, birds molt their feathers regularly, shedding and replacing them symmetrically, and usually a few at a time, to maintain maximum efficiency. Some ducks and geese,

however, drop all their flight feathers at once and are unable to fly until new ones grow. Most birds, though, shed their feathers one by one in a regular, fixed sequence. Watch flying birds and look for gaps in the shape of the wing, or for new, fresh, dark feathers growing among paler, rough-edged, old ones.

Replacing feathers consumes a lot of energy, and molt must therefore occur when energy-rich foods are readily available and when the bird is not involved in other energy-sapping activities. It is no accident that the complete annual molt of birds occurs after breeding and usually before migration.

Not only does molting refresh a bird's plumage, it can also change a bird's appearance according to age and season. Dull-brown young birds, for example, become brighter as they gain adult feathers. Drab winter plumage can be changed for brighter breeding plumages. It is not always so simple: ducks, for example, pair up in winter and look brightest in the coldest months. In summer, the male loses his ability to fly and molts into a faded, dark pattern—called "eclipse" plumage—so that he is more camouflaged and less likely to fall prey to a passing hawk or fox.

Birds' Bills

The bills of birds occur in a tremendous range of shapes, reflecting the adaptation of each species to its unique mode of obtaining food. Many birds also have specially shaped or colored bills that they use in courtship rituals.

COMMON RAVEN

The raven uses its heavy, arched, powerful bill for all-round foraging and tearing up tough items before eating.

ICTERINE WARBLER

Shallow but broad, this bird's bill is shaped for seizing insects.

CHANNEL-BILLED TOUCAN

This bird has a remarkable bill, which is very large but extremely lightweight, for reaching fruits on thin twigs.

A bird's bill consists of an upper jaw, which is fixed on the skull and almost immobile, and a lower jaw that is articulated like ours and opens to reveal a wide gape.

Hornlike sheaths

Each jaw has a bony base. The lower base is formed by two bones, which are fused together where they meet near the tip of the bill. The space between them is filled by the soft throat and chin (or sometimes a fleshy pouch). These bones are covered by hard, hornlike—or sometimes leathery—sheaths that give the bill its detailed shape.

On a few birds, such as the puffin, the sheaths are shed or modified after the breeding season, allowing for marked differences in the size of the bill, according to the season. In most birds, seasonal changes are limited to alterations in color. On birds such as herons, these color changes can be brief but rapid, with a visible increase in the intensity of color during periods of excitement in spring courtship.

Flexible bills

While the upper jaw is fixed, the tip of the long upper jaw extending from the skull can be surprisingly flexible. Even birds such as cormorants can raise the upper bill to an unexpected degree in a wide "yawn." Snipe and woodcock have especially sensitive bills, and they can detect prey while probing deep in soft mud or soil. Once a worm has been found, by touch, the bill is flexible enough to allow the tip to open and grasp the prey, which can then be swallowed without a pause in the deep probing.

Seed-eaters' bills

Sparrows and finches have broad, deep, triangular bills for feeding on hard seeds. They vary, nevertheless. A goldfinch has a fine, pointed, triangle-shaped bill for probing into complex flower heads such as thistles for seeds. The bill of a crossbill is literally crossed at the tip, which allows it to reach inside of the scales of pine and larch cones to extract the seeds within with its tongue. Most finches have "middle-sized" triangular bills for crushing tough seeds, and their bills have sharp cutting edges to de-husk them. At a feeder you can often watch a finch manipulating a seed with its bill and tongue, peeling off the outer husk and nibbling at the kernel within.

Insect-eaters' fine tools

Insect-eating birds such as warblers have fine, narrow bills for picking tiny prey from twigs and foliage. Flycatchers have broader bills, often fringed with stiff bristles, and wide mouths so they can catch insects in flight. Swifts and nightjars have minute bills, but huge mouths, which open wide to catch insects in the air. But many birds have "all rounder" bills, and even sparrows can catch insects when they wish to, and scoop up vast numbers of aphids when feeding their young.

Starlings have stout, strong, pointed bills with especially adapted muscles that they use to probe into grass and open their bills to get at the larvae of chafers and other prey. A thrush has a stronger bill than a warbler, and it is longer and more slender than a sparrow's: they eat worms, grubs, seeds, and all kinds of fruit. Its bill is more of a tool for all trades than a specialized instrument.

GREEN WOODPECKER
The dagger-shaped, chisel-like bill of this bird is used for digging into ant-hills and chipping out nesting cavities in tree branches.

NORTHERN CARDINAL
This bird has a thick, triangular seed-eater's bill.

BLUE-AND-YELLOW MACAW
The deep, arched, hook-tipped bill of this bird is used to rip open fruits and seed pods.

GOLDEN EAGLE

Typical for a bird of prey, this eagle has a hooked bill, which is used for tearing apart meaty foods.

GIANT HUMMINGBIRD

This bill is specialized for taking nectar from flowers and snatching tiny insects.

COMMON REDSHANK

The slim, sensitive bill of this bird can probe into wet mud and sand.

Hooked and toothed bills

Birds of prey have a hook-tipped bill, also known as a beak, for tearing prey apart. Few of these birds capture prey in their beak—they normally use their feet to snatch their victims—but many kill prey with a sharp bite. A falcon's beak has a small "tooth" on the sheath of the upper bill to help sever the neck of a mouse or small bird. Vultures have bills that are designed for the food in their local area: the big Black and Griffon Vultures (true members of the Falconiformes) of Europe have heavy bills that can tear into the hide of dead animals, while the Turkey Vulture of the Americas (related to storks) and the Egyptian Vulture of southern Europe (another Falconiform bird) have narrow, fine bills for probing deep inside carcasses made of weaker tissue.

Other birds also have hooked bills. Parrots are primarily fruit and seed eaters, and their thick, hooked bills allow them to cope with large fruit and seed pods. Mergansers not only have hooks, but also tooth-like edges to the bill, to keep a firm grip on slippery, muscular fish. Gannets, kingfishers, herons, and egrets manage to eat their fish diet quite well without either feature, grasping prey in their powerful, pointed, sharp-edged bills before turning them to swallow the fish head-first so there is no risk of choking on extended spines or fins.

Probes and hammers

Shorebird bills are greatly adapted to habitat and food preferences. Curlews have down-curved bills, perhaps so they can easily see what they are doing with the bill's fine tip. But they also probe and twist the bill, and the curve might allow them a better chance to detect prey. Godwits, snipe, and dowitchers, however, probe adequately with long, straight bills.

Plovers take food from the shore, often on mudflats, using a shorter, thicker bill; a Dunlin picks from, or just beneath, the surface of mud and sand with a longer, fine-tipped bill. A turnstone has a strong, slightly up-curved bill that it uses to move pebbles and seaweed in search of hidden invertebrates. An avocet's up-curved bill is swept sideways through shallow water to capture prey near the surface, while a spoonbill's broad bill with its wide, flattened tip is swept—slightly open—from side to side through the water until a fish is touched and the bill grabs it as with a pair of salad tongs.

Oystercatchers can have a pointed bill, used to slip inside shellfish to cut the muscle that holds the shells tight together, or a blunt-tipped bill, which is used to hammer the shells to pieces.

RED-BREASTED MERGANSER
With serrated edges for grasping fish, this is a typical sawbill duck's bill.

MALLARD
This bird uses its broad bill for "dabbling" in shallow water to pick up seeds and aquatic creatures.

AMERICAN DARTER
This fish-catcher bill can grab or stab fish.

Birds' Feet

Birds rely not only on their wings to get around—they use their feet for walking. Their feet are adapted for walking styles as well as for gripping tasks, whether it be an eagle snatching a fish or a robin perching in a tree.

COMMON PHEASANT

The strong, stubby feet of this bird are adapted for walking.

CARRION CROW

This bird has strong feet adapted for perching and walking.

NORTHERN JACANA

The exceptionally long toes of the jacana help to spread its weight on floating leaves.

Most birds have four toes, three pointing forward and one backward, to allow for a good grip on a perch, such as a twig or branch. Small songbirds that walk or run on the ground, such as larks and pipits, have a very long hind claw. Some larger birds that walk or run in open places have only three toes, with the hind toe lost or reduced to a stub.

The hind toe is also much reduced in ducks, geese, swans, and gulls; instead, the front three toes are joined by leathery webs that give a stronger push against water for more powerful swimming. Gannets, pelicans, cormorants, and their relatives reveal their close relationship by their feet, on which broad webs join all four toes.

Falcons have strong toes and sharp, arched claws, with which they grasp their prey. Bird-eating harriers and hawks have longer legs, much longer toes, and needle-sharp, curved claws that enable them to capture birds in flight and kill them by puncturing vital organs.

ROCK PTARMIGAN

Feathered toes give this bird better insulation in snow.

GREEN WOODPECKER

The outer toe of this species splays outward and backward to give good grip on a rounded branch.

HOUSE SPARROW

Typical for perching birds, the sparrow has three toes pointing forward and one back.

AMERICAN HARPY EAGLE

Its huge feet, strong toes, and arched, sharp claws enable this bird to kill large prey such as monkeys.

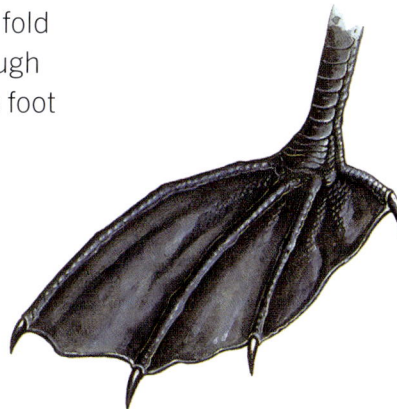

Waders

Shorebirds may have very long legs for wading in shallow water. Plovers have just three toes, while sandpipers have four, longer, more slender toes. Avocet toes are joined by partial webs. Similarly, rails and crakes may have very long, slim toes to take their weight on soft mud and floating vegetation—yet the closely related coots have broad lobes along each side of each toe, as do the grebes. These fold flat when the foot is pushed forward through water, reducing drag, but open out as the foot is pushed back, to give forward thrust.

GREAT CORMORANT

All four toes of this bird are joined by webs to provide powerful underwater propulsion.

BLACK COOT

The lobes on this bird's toes spread out on back stroke and fold away on forward stroke for efficient swimming.

OSTRICH

Its feet are designed for long-distance walking and running at great speed.

GREY HERON

Its long legs and toes allow this heron to wade in the shallows and stand on soft mud without sinking.

COLORS AND PATTERNS

Feathers occur in just about any color variation you can think of. Their patterns and colors can be amazingly complex. Yet many birds have a basic similarity, especially within families.

Remarkable consistency

If you look at 10,000 Black-headed Gulls at a reservoir roost, there will be almost no variation among them in the color of their upperparts: all are the same pale, silvery-gray. Watch the thrushes in your garden and, year after year, they will each have exactly the same shade of brown on the back. There are individual differences, but the essential truth is that birds of one species are usually amazingly alike.

This helps bird-watchers, because it makes the birds easier to identify. Variation within a species is often linked to geography. When one species has a wide geographic range, those at one end can be a little—or, rarely, a lot—different from those at the other. In many geographically variable species, there is a smooth gradient of variation (such as in size or color) from one extreme of the range to another. Such a smooth gradient is called a "cline."

Differences according to age

While most young birds look a little unlike their parents, sometimes the differences can be striking. Young gulls are mostly drab, mottled brown, and quite unlike their sharp parents. They need to stay hidden, and their brown color provides good camouflage—an adult will treat another individual in adult plumage as a potential competitor and will react aggressively toward it. It will react differently to a bird in juvenile plumage, however, recognizing that it is only a juvenile and poses no threat.

Differences according to sex

Many species, including wrens, Blue Jays, Red-headed Woodpeckers, and some thrushes, have males and females that are identical. Others have marked sexual differences: Northern Cardinal, Eastern Towhee, most woodpeckers, ducks and gamebirds, such as pheasants,

NORTHERN SHOVELER

There is no discernible difference between the shades of rusty-red, dark green, brown, and blue on shovelers found across the Northern Hemisphere.

are good examples. In some polygamous species, such as Ruffs and Ruffed or Sage Grouse, males display together in spring so that females can choose the best mates. In Ruffs, the difference in color is heightened in spring, but in other species, such as pheasants and peacocks, the difference remains all year round.

Differences according to season

Spring and summer see many male birds at their finest: they are in breeding or courtship plumage. During this time of year they need to impress females and also ward off rival males without having to fight—they can do so by looking brighter, fitter, and more dominant than their rivals.

A Black-headed Gull gains its hood in late winter; the dark hood develops from the back of the head forward so that it is complete, and most intimidating to rivals, by early spring. The brilliance of wildfowl males, such as goldeneyes, Mallards, and mergansers, is best seen in the winter, when the sexes pair up, often before they migrate north to breeding areas. Yet geese, which are closely related to wildfowl, have no obvious differences between male and female during the summer or winter. There is clearly no "right" way to use color and pattern, and there are many different strategies that work for different species.

Camouflage

Birds do not have the ability to camouflage themselves as well as insects that look like leaves or fish that look like seaweed. They must be able to fly and live active lives, so they rely on their colors and patterns, rather than outlines, to help them hide. But some birds have developed wonderful camouflage: woodcocks blend in with dead leaves on

KINGFISHER

Many colorful birds rely on the structure of their feathers to separate white light and produce brilliant hues, rather like the pits on a compact disc.

the forest floor, and grouse blend into their heathery backgrounds exceedingly well. Many birds the world over have darker feathers on the back than on the belly. The natural tendency for a bird's upperside to be lit by stronger light and the underside to be in shade helps "flatten out" the bird's colors and makes it more difficult to see it. Look at a thrush or robin and you will see that the flank—just where the sun tends to catch the fluffed out feathers—tends to be a little darker than the belly. This pattern of dark above and light below is known as countershading.

Showing off

Swans are so big and so strong that they really have no need for camouflage. Instead, they are dazzlingly white and brilliantly obvious to other swans from a mile away. This simple statement communicates their presence to all other birds.

White plumage is used in other ways, too. Gannets plunge from a height to catch fish. If one dives, the rest notice the bright white bird creating a big white splash, and they hone in on the spot, congregating rapidly above a shoal of fish. Colors and patterns are used to display aggression, too. A robin spreads its red breast feathers to antagonize other robins. Usually such a show of strength and fitness is enough to avoid a fight: the bright color helps reduce the need for more drastic action

FOOD AND FEEDING

The great diversity of birds is largely due to the many different kinds of foods that they can exploit, along with the variety of their habitats and the isolation of species by geographic barriers. Most species of birds are adapted to feed on something very slightly different from their close neighbors, so that competition for prey is kept low.

In general, birds eat feverishly early in the morning after having fasted all night. Then they rest, feed casually during the day, then feed feverishly again before going to roost for the night.

Food from the trees

Brown Creepers feed on minute insects and spiders, including their eggs and larvae, on the bark of trees. They explore the tiniest crevices using their thin, curved bills. Nuthatches also explore the bark but are more likely to take larger food and eat far more seeds and berries. They have stronger feet for a better grip, which makes them more agile, and bigger bills to tackle larger food items—they can even hammer open tough nuts.

COMMON SNIPE

The bill is flexible but strong enough to open underground and grasp a worm.

Chickadees and titmice also explore tree bark and foliage. The Tufted Titmouse tends to prefer the bark of the trunks and bigger branches of trees, as well as finding food on the ground below, while smaller chickadees feed on slimmer branches and twigs, looking for smaller prey. In this way, these different species can move together as a flock, keeping their eyes open for possible danger, while keeping out of each other's way and eating different food.

Chickadees find an abundance of food at different times of the year and hide a lot of it by pushing it into places that they are likely to search again later, such as bunches of pine needles. These stores of food can then be saved for the winter. While chickadees find stored food again by chance, various crows, jays, and magpies locate their stored food by design. They bury nuts, scraps of meat, and acorns and can remember where they put their winter stores months later.

Beneath the surface

Shorebirds feed in rhythm with the tides, so their feeding times fluctuate from day to day, always coming at low tide. Wading birds on a beach use different feeding strategies too. A Semipalmated (with toes webbed for part of their length) Plover picks small shellfish and crustaceans from the surface of the mud, while a Semipalmated Sandpiper or a Dunlin picks from an abundance of minute snails

FLYCATCHER

While warblers mostly have fine, thin bills, flycatchers have broader bills with bristles around them, making it easier to snap-up flying insects.

barely hidden in the wet mud at low tide. A Red Knot has a longer bill and probes a little more deeply. Godwits probe deeper still for small worms, while curlews, which have very long bills, probe deep down for bigger lugworms, as well as taking ragworms, shellfish, and small crabs from rock pools as the tide falls. Each in its own way is adapted to feed on different food, or in different situations, so that all can live together on the same beach.

Climate change

Many seed-eating birds, such as finches and sparrows, need to eat insects during the summer. The adult birds manage to survive on only seeds, but their fast-growing chicks must have energy-rich, high-protein food, and the best source is insect food. Finches feed thousands of leaf-eating caterpillars to their young in the nest. Recently, tits have had poorer breeding seasons, and this may be because they are nesting at the "usual" time, while their caterpillar food is emerging two or three weeks earlier due to the effects of climate change. Global warming is wreaking havoc in some places as the reproductive cycles of birds and their prey are becoming out of sync.

NO CONTEST

A remarkable means of avoiding competition is seen in birds of prey, especially in bird-eating hawks, such as Cooper's and Sharp-shinned Hawks—the female is up to one-third bigger than the male. This means that the sexes eat prey of different sizes and so do not compete with one another, allowing them to survive together in a smaller area without straining the supply of food.

How to Feed Birds in the Garden

Feeding garden birds has become a multi-million dollar business. The trend began in North America and followed later on in Europe. Today, the new foods that are being used in bird feeders are attracting different kinds of birds, and present the food in ever more sophisticated ways.

Bird lovers feed garden birds for two main reasons: to help birds survive in a tougher environment, and to see them up close. Fortunately, the two are mutually beneficial.

Positioning a feeder
To get a good view of birds feeding in your garden, the feeder must be placed so that you can see it from a normal position within the house. A feeding tray must be high enough that you can easily see it while sitting down in a favorite comfortable chair. It is no use if it is hidden below the window level.

The feeder should be placed away from any cold, windy channel between walls or buildings—a little shelter is always welcome. It is also a good idea to position it away from a footpath, where the birds may be disturbed.

Any feeder is vulnerable to predation: if you put out foods to attract birds, you will attract hawks and other predators, too. A bird feeder covered in tits provides an easy meal for a hawk. There is no way to eliminate this danger, but you can do things to minimize the risk. The most effective solution is a dome of large-mesh chicken wire placed over the feeder, which will allow smaller birds to enter while keeping predators out. Netting is likely to be chewed through by squirrels. Suspending unwanted CDs from loose strings on the feeder may distract both hawks and the songbirds you want to attract—but this deterrent will not last.

If you place a feeder close to a bush or tree, it gives small birds a sporting chance of diving to safety. On the other hand, positioning a feeder by thick shrubbery or a flowerbed might invite unwanted attention from the local cat, the garden bird's greatest enemy.

When to feed birds
You can feed birds all year round. Birds need food in winter to help them survive the cold nights, but spring can also be a difficult time for them. Those that rely on seeds and fruit can find that natural supplies are at their lowest ebb by late spring and a free handout of birdseeds and peanuts can be a real boost just before the breeding season.

DIFFERENT TECHNIQUES
Try putting fat and cheese in crevices in tree bark, and scatter grated cheese under bushes for shy birds that don't come to tables. Feeding birds in several places will attract a greater number and variety, and allow birds to feed without constantly squabbling.

KEEP IT NATURAL

It is vital to include natural bird foods in your garden and to have a variety of plants that can provide them. House sparrows are declining fast in many parts of the world. In winter, they have fewer seeds to eat as herbicides have reduced the number of weeds and high-tech harvesting has minimized the spillage of grain. In summer, they are unable to rear young, because pesticides and low-maintenance gardens with fewer shrubs mean a lack of insects.

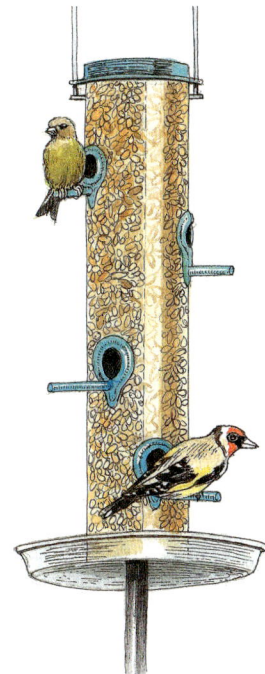

FEEDER TYPES

Rigid spiral metal feeders (above left) are safe, but springy ones may trap birds' feet. Solid-mesh feeders (above center) are ideal for bulky foods; special tubes (above right) are needed for finer seeds.

Remember that young birds are being fed in the nest during spring and summer. Although most birds will not feed their chicks food that might endanger them, if natural food is scarce, they may resort to feeding them foods such as peanuts. Baby birds can choke on large peanuts, so make sure they are crushed and crumbled, or wrap them in a strong mesh that is fine enough to make birds peck pieces from them, rather than take them away whole.

Types of feeders

Do not use flexible feeders. One neat design is the coil spring feeder with a base and lid—but make sure the coil is very rigid. A flexible coil may catch the legs and feet of feeding birds and injure or kill them. Peanuts have long been sold in plastic mesh bags, which can be hung outside as ready-made feeders. These are generally fine to use, but increasingly people have become aware that they can trap and kill small birds. Birds can get their feet and even their tongue tangled in the mesh so that they hang from it until they die. It is best to avoid such bags and instead place the nuts inside a rigid metal mesh basket or a plastic tube with special feeding ports.

Foods to Offer Birds

Feeding birds in a garden can be great fun: you can experiment with different foods and the way you offer them. There are types of bird foods available to suit every budget, from expensive seeds to cheap kitchen scraps. Just remember to keep everything clean. Piles of old bird droppings or decaying food can promote disease and wipe out the very birds you are trying to save.

Plant shrubs and herbs—especially species native to your area—in the garden to help birds find food. Many of these plants provide nectar and attract insects, which birds eat. Others produce fruits—all kinds of berry-bearing shrubs are excellent for birds, especially cotoneasters, berberis, and hawthorns, as well as pyracantha and holly. Such natural foods are good for birds and keep a natural balance in the garden.

If you have feeders and a birdtable, or a ground feeder, you can do a great deal to help birds. They need energy, which often means fat: full-fat cheese, cooked bacon rind, suet, and animal fats make perfect foods and can also form the basis of "bird cakes."

To make a bird cake, use the fatty material to bind together nuts, seeds, fruits, and scraps. Squeeze or pour the mixture into containers such as yogurt pots and coconut shells. Hung in trees or from the birdtable, these are great feeders that offer food for winter birds. Do not put such fat-based foods out in the summer heat. The fat melts and can cause feather damage and loss as the oils soak into the bird's plumage.

The right foods
Bread is a good type of food to provide birds in small quantities. Brown, damp bread is preferable—dry, crusty bread is often neglected. Stale cake crumbled on the birdtable or on the ground is often a better choice. Kitchen scraps of all kinds, from uncooked or cooked pastry to bits of fruit, will usually be accepted.

Apples also make good food, especially if they are cut into small pieces or halved and scattered on the ground for thrushes, or put on the birdtable. Scatter them in several places if you have space, so that a number of birds can feed without fighting.

Peanuts are a popular, traditional food for birds and remain ideal, especially for tits when hung in a mesh or special tubular feeder—but many finches and other birds will eat them, too. Woodpeckers often find them and come frequently to feed on them.

Sunflower seeds are excellent, oily food for birds such as the larger finches, and are a great alternative to peanuts. Smaller finches will also eat oats and millet scattered on the ground or a table or placed in a feeder. Nyjer, or niger, seed is a much finer seed that requires special feeders. It may not work, but when it does, it can attract goldfinches and siskins and keep dozens of them coming back for weeks. It is, however, quite expensive.

 Wild bird seeds come in many mixtures, from cheap seeds to pricey high-protein mixes. Cheaper seeds have a lot of large grains, which are not eaten by many birds other than pigeons, and may even be padded out for bulk with substances such as broken dog

FEEDING TIPS

When you feed the birds, take the following steps to provide a safe and healthy feeding environment.

- Position feeding stations in different areas of your yard to spread birds around and avoid competition, stress, and disease.

- Clean your feeders regularly with hot water, and let them dry completely. Keep areas under and around the feeders clean.

- Keep seed clean and dry and watch that it doesn't get moldy. If there is a lot of waste, reduce the amount of food you put out.

- Use a seed blend that is designed for the feeder you have and the type of birds that come to that feeder.

- Offer seeds in a feeder rather than scattering seed on the ground.

- If possible, move your feeding stations periodically, so there will be less concentration of bird droppings.

- Always wash your hands after filling or cleaning your feeders.

- Place bird feeders in locations that do not provide hiding places where cats and other predators can wait to ambush the feeder. Bird feeders should be placed 5–12 inches (12.5–30 cm) from low shrubs or bushes that provide cover.

- Place the feeder 5–12 feet (1.5–3.5 m) from a brush pile or bushes to provide a place for birds to take cover in the event of danger.

biscuit. Try to choose better quality foods from reputable sources.

Don't feed birds salted foods, such as salted peanuts, potato chips, or salty bacon. Also avoid giving desiccated coconut and other dried foods that may swell after they are swallowed.

Water

Fresh water is vital for birds, all year round: even in the depths of winter they need to drink and they need to bathe. Put out a dish or fill a birdbath each day. Keep the water clean, and never use any artificial substances to prevent the water from freezing.

Hygiene

Cleanliness is important for birds and every bit as vital for you. Use rubber gloves when handling feeders and cleaning tables; use a stiff brush and keep it solely for the purpose of cleaning your birdtable. Move your feeders around every so often to avoid a buildup of droppings and waste. Now and then, wash them in a weak solution of ordinary bleach and rinse them clean.

NESTS

The main purpose of any bird is to reproduce and ensure the survival of its species: to do so, it must find a mate, and females must nest, lay eggs, and see that their chicks are reared. A nest is simply a receptacle—or even a mere scrape in the ground—in which the eggs are laid and incubated until they hatch.

EARTH NEST

Terns, gulls, and wading birds lay their eggs in a scraped hollow in earth or sand.

EAGLE NEST

Many big birds of prey reuse big stick nests, which can become enormous over many years.

In many species the young remain in the nest until they can fly. Once the nest has fulfilled its purpose—by which time it may be an unsavory and unhygienic place containing various parasites, droppings, and uneaten scraps of food—it is usually neglected. Some larger species, however, build more substantial nests, which are refurbished year after year—the nests built by eagles and Ospreys may become very large.

Nest uses

A nest is the place where a bird lays its eggs and incubates them until they hatch. It is not a "home" used by birds at other times, although some hole nests are used as roosting sites in winter. A nest or nest site may be used many times over, or a new one may be made for each set of eggs. In general, small birds use new nests for each clutch during a season, as the nest becomes a dirty and unhygienic place after rearing a family: it tends to harbor many parasites, such as mites, ticks, and fleas, probably has waste food in and around it, and is soiled with droppings. Larger birds, which have just one clutch each year, are more likely to reuse a nest in successive seasons, provided at least one of the pair survives: in some species, such as Ospreys and Golden Eagles, nests may be used by generations of birds over decades, and others, such as Peregrine Falcons and ravens, use the same piece of cliff, if not the same ledge, for many years.

Birds with no nest

Not all species build a structure for the nest: some simply lay eggs directly onto the bare ground, onto a cliff ledge, or inside a hole, without any nest material being added. Kingfishers lay onto a bare floor inside a deep tunnel, but as the eggs hatch and the young grow, their nest chamber fills with bits of fish and undigested fish bones, as well as foul, semi-liquid droppings.

Some birds such as guillemots and other seabirds, and Peregrine Falcons, lay eggs on a bare ledge, or at best a scrape in earth or gravel naturally collected on a cliff ledge. Hygiene here is also suspect: seabirds in colonies may be splashed with droppings from birds on ledges higher up the cliff. Birds of prey, however, while they may build up unwanted food that simply rots around the nest, usually at least keep the

WOODPECKER NEST

Even firm, healthy wood can be chipped away by a woodpecker as it excavates its round, deep nesting hole.

LEDGE NEST

Some birds of prey, including Peregrine Falcons, nest on earthy ledges on the face of cliffs.

nest free from droppings, and the young birds quickly learn to back up to the side of the nest and void their excreta over the edge. Other birds, such as plovers, add a few scraps of vegetation, shells, or stones to a scrape on the ground or in a sandy beach and the addition of such objects can become ritualized.

Nest materials

While falcons make no nest, hawks do so, usually in trees. Eagles and Ospreys can build up huge nests using sticks, which accumulate over decades of repeated use, creating incredible structures on cliffs, poles, or in treetops. They also bring green foliage to the nest all summer, perhaps to help keep down flies and pests in a nest full of rolling food.

In those birds that do build nests, often both sexes share the work, but the female may add the final lining. In many cases the male makes the initial foundations. Male wrens make several nests as part of their courtship routine:

SONGBIRD NEST

A typical small bird's nest is a cup-shaped structure, often with a softer lining.

they attract females and show them a choice of nests, perching nearby and waving their wings as they encourage the female to inspect each site, but the female makes the final choice of which one to use.

Many nests are simple structures of sticks and twigs, usually with a lining of smaller materials and perhaps feathers, hair, or fine plant fibers. Such a nest made by a small songbird can be completed within two days: other more complex structures may take a week or two to complete. Magpies add a protective dome to their "fortress" nests. Small songbirds make more complex structures, usually cup-shaped, with a softer lining; those of the thrushes, such as American Robins and the European Blackbird, have a strong, hard mud layer inside a basic structure of grasses and twigs. Some, such as the Long-tailed Tit's nest, or the smaller, hammock-like nests of Goldcrests and kinglets, are beautiful, delicate, and made of lichens and moss held together with spider's webs. These nests stretch as the brood of chicks grows. Wildfowl pluck down from their own bodies to add a warm, soft layer to the inside of the nest.

Hole nests

Many birds nest in holes of some kind: woodpeckers chip out a hole in a tree, while kingfishers dig into an earth bank. Birds as varied as chickadees and tits, owls, and kestrels occupy a hole in a tree—either a natural hole or one made by a woodpecker. Nuthatches of several species plaster up the entrance hole with mud, until it is just big enough to allow them in, but excludes larger predators. They will also plaster mud between a nest box and the bole of a tree, which perhaps insulates the box and provides greater stability. The plastering habit is probably simply instinctive and used whether it has a necessary function or not: nuthatches cannot resist doing it.

Artificial nests

Birds that nest in holes can be helped, even in gardens, by the use of artificial nest boxes. In the U.K., Blue and Great Tits are common nest box occupants, while populations of Pied Flycatchers have been increased in many woodlands by the provision of boxes where natural holes are few. In the U.S.A., Purple Martins will use large "apartment house" boxes on special poles, and bluebirds can be helped by the provision of boxes in and around gardens. Special boxes can be used by owls and kestrels, while artificial structures that provide shelter for chicks have helped rare birds such as Roseate Terns improve their breeding success on nature reserves, where severe weather and predators otherwise take their toll.

Nest boxes

Nest boxes can easily be made to standard sizes and designs from wood, or "woodcrete"—a mixture of sawdust and cement—which helps to protect eggs and chicks from the attentions of woodpeckers and other predators that can gain access to a normal wooden box. While metal shields around the entrance may deter some predators, woodpeckers can still dig their way in from the side unless a more resilient material is used.

NEST BOX

These structures can be made in many shapes and sizes according to the bird you have in mind: this one would suit a small hole-nester.

TENEMENT BLOCKS

The Purple Martin has been exclusively nesting in this style of nest box for nearly a century in the eastern part of North America.

SONG, COURTSHIP, AND DISPLAY

During the spring, a territorial bird (usually a male, but sometimes a female or a pair) has to find a territory that will support himself, a mate, and their young. Birds use song to attract a mate, repel rivals, or both. Courtship involves ritualized displays that help break down a bird's instinct to maintain individual distance and strengthen a pair bond. Such displays often have different meanings from species to species.

LAPWING

This shorebird combines striking colors and shapes, distinctive calls, and a wild, tumbling flight in its displays.

By singing, a male bird tells other males that an area is occupied—it is a clear message that provides birds with space that is free of competition and interference—and the space usually comes as a result of song rather than potentially injurious physical conflict.

Song

Songs are specific to each species. Basic songs, such as a wren's, are simple and have little variation. Longer, more sophisticated songs develop with age as the bird adds to its repertoire, to show how mature and experienced it is. A rich variety of songs is used by the Marsh Warbler in the U.K. and the Northern Mockingbird in North America, which add to their repertoire by imitating a vast range of other birds—maybe 100 or more. The Marsh Warbler even includes mimicry of birds it encounters in its winter in Africa. The reason for this behavior is unknown—in males, it may be simply a method of displaying virtuosity to the females. At the other end of the scale, a young bird deprived of hearing others of its species will grow up using an ordinary, simple, "low-quality" version of its species song, reflecting the song's inherited nature but also the influence of competition with and imitation of others. If two birds that have not yet claimed a territory both want to settle in the same area, and both have a more or less equal interest in and access to it, they may fight ferociously. Male birds generally fight other males, and females fight other females—sometimes, but rarely, to the death. If two males are both settled in their own territories and meet at the boundary between them, they will call, sing, and display to avoid fighting. If one bird trespasses, the other, defending, bird will usually manage to drive it away.

Courtship

In many songbirds, and some other birds such as terns, the male feeds the female during courtship and early in the breeding season. Such courtship feeding aids in pair bonding, but also helps the female survive a period of stress, when she is using huge amounts of energy to lay a large clutch of eggs.

Display

In large birds of prey, such as larger hawks and eagles, aerial displays take the place of song. Sounds do not carry far in the huge territories of these birds, but they can see each other from great distances. These birds spend hours soaring over their nesting areas so that others of their species can see, and keep away.

Not all birds form long-lasting pair bonds when breeding. Game birds such as grouse and pheasants are polygynous, meaning that one male mates with two or more females; the males fight and show off but it is the females that select a mate. Such fights and displays are highly ritualized, and often take place at traditional sites that have been used for decades. Black Grouse in Europe and Greater Prairie Chickens in

North America, for example, collect in spring at a place called a "lek." The males strut, spread their tails, jump in the air, make special sounds, and occasionally fight. The females look on, deciding which is the "best" male to father their young.

WILD TURKEY

A big, healthy turkey is an impressive sight even to us. Its performance must impress both rivals and potential mates.

HOW BIRDS SING

Feeding birds in a garden can be great fun: you can experiment with different foods and the way you offer them. There are types of bird foods available to suit every budget, from expensive seeds to cheap kitchen scraps. Just remember to keep everything clean. Piles of old bird droppings or decaying food can promote disease and wipe out the very birds you are trying to save.

The vocal sounds produced by birds are made in a completely different manner than those produced by mammals. Instead of having a larynx with vocal cords situated at the top of the trachea, birds possess an organ called the syrinx. This is a V-shaped structure situated at the base of the trachea (windpipe) where it divides into two bronchi that run to the lungs. Inside the syrinx are thin tympanic membranes that vibrate when air passes over them as it escapes from the lungs. The shape of the syrinx can be altered by muscles attached to

it. This in turn changes the shape and tension of the tympanic membranes, which then varies the pitch of the sound produced. The more muscles to control the syrinx, the richer the range of sound. Songbirds have from five to nine, which give them their wide vocal abilities.

Variations on a Theme
Of songbird species, ovenbirds, wood creepers, and antbirds (the suboscines) have the most primitive type of syrinx, with the membranes attached only to the trachea. The rest of

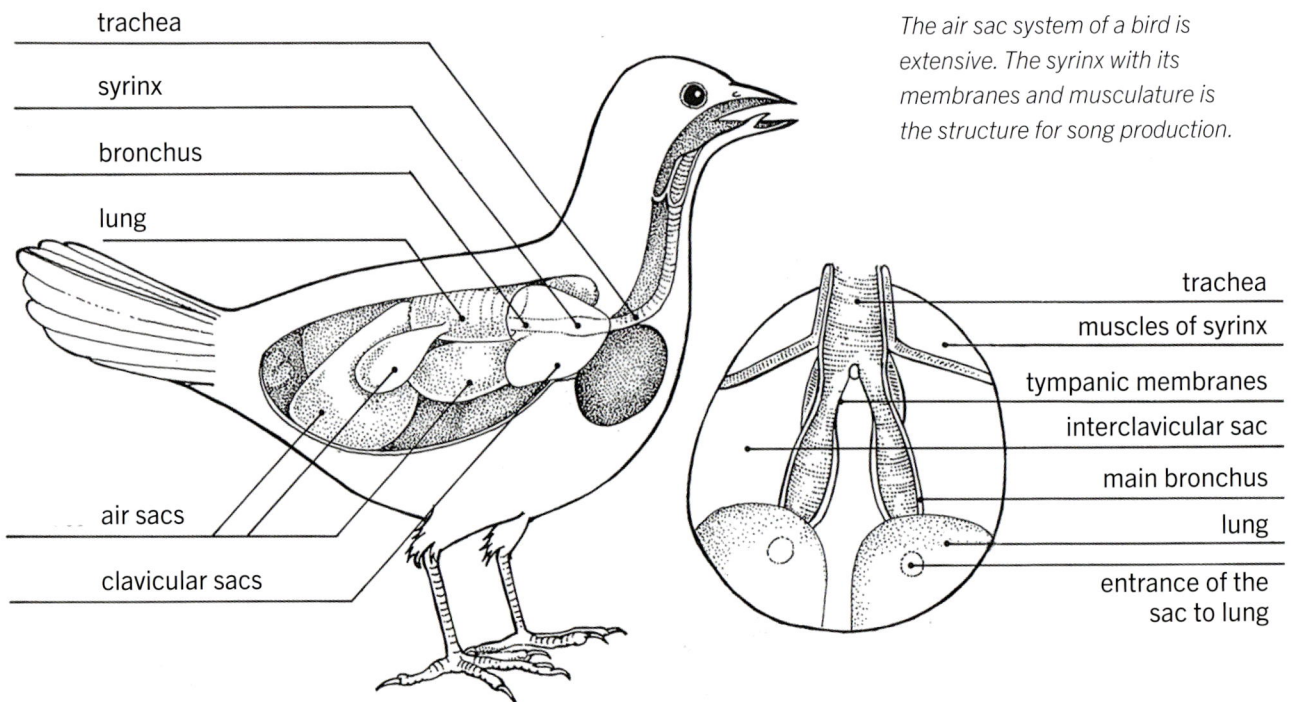

trachea
syrinx
bronchus
lung
air sacs
clavicular sacs

The air sac system of a bird is extensive. The syrinx with its membranes and musculature is the structure for song production.

trachea
muscles of syrinx
tympanic membranes
interclavicular sac
main bronchus
lung
entrance of the sac to lung

the songbirds have membranes that can be attached to both the trachea and bronchi in different ways.

Part of a bird's respiratory system is formed by a series of air sacs; these allow a greater volume of air to be taken in than the lungs alone would hold. The interclavicular air sac surrounds the syrinx and exerts pressure on it. This particular air sac is essential for the production of sounds; if ruptured, no sounds can be made. The trachea also plays a role by acting as a resonance chamber.

Among the different bird species, there is a great variation in syrinx structure and, therefore, the types of sound produced. The length and width of the trachea also play a part in the final sound. A short, narrow trachea produces a higher resonance than a short, broad trachea. As song originates from the base of the trachea, it is possible for birds to sing with their bills full of food, or even closed.

Unusual sounds

Some species, not noted for their songs, use their air sacs to produce extraordinary sounds. Greater and lesser prairie chickens inflate theirs to produce a booming sound, and the sacs can be seen stretching the bare neck skin as they are inflated. Pigeons inflate their esophagus with air to give their characteristic cooing tone. The modification of syrinx, trachea, and air sacs is what makes birdsong so beautifully varied and unique.

Many birds — though relatively few songbirds —— produce sounds other than vocal noises by using parts of their bodies. Hummingbirds are so-called because of the noise their wings make, and the varying species each produce a different hum. Other parts of the body can be used to produce sounds. Storks clap their bills together to make a loud rattling sound, and woodpeckers drum with their bills against a tree or branch.

Mimicry

There are some species where the majority of the song appears to be innate. Song sparrows, for instance, do not need to hear a parent or any other song sparrow to develop a perfect song pattern. When they do hear one, however, they develop a song that mimics the song sparrow dialect they hear. As a result, song sparrows may have as many as 50 distinct local dialects.

As well as learning their own songs, many birds are excellent mimics, building the phrases of other species into their own songs. The Indian hill mynah is an accomplished mimic in captivity, to the extent that it can even copy human speech; in the wild, however, it does not incorporate the songs of other birds into its own. The marsh warbler breeds in Europe and winters in Africa, and its song is made up almost entirely of phrases from other species. Studies have shown that these consist of a mixture of phrases from nearly 100 European species and over 100 African species. The most notable North American mimic is the mockingbird, known to imitate 55 species in an hour.

When Birds Sing

In temperate regions, the amount of daylight plays an important part in the life of all birds. It tells migrants when to migrate, and it also triggers the production of hormones that prepare birds for the breeding season. Singing is stimulated by the presence of the male sex hormone, testosterone, produced when daylight length reaches a certain amount — usually in excess of 12 hours. In temperate regions, this results in a distinct breeding season during which the majority of birds breed. In the tropics, where the change in day length is minimal, other factors may also be responsible, which is why breeding occurs throughout the year in such areas. As birdsong is linked so closely to breeding, most singing takes place during the breeding season.

The length of song period varies from species to species, and the timing of the breeding season differs geographically. Birds that breed in temperate regions have a clearly defined breeding season. Many birds begin singing in earnest at the beginning of the year, so as to establish their territories early on. As spring approaches, more and more birds sing, and with the arrival of spring migrants the chorus is complete. In the northern hemisphere, there is nothing to compare with the woodland dawn chorus in early May.

For the most part, spring visitors will have been silent on their wintering grounds, but as they prepare to migrate they often begin to sing. The song begins very tentatively to start with, and far from perfect; many young birds will be singing for the first time. When these migrants eventually reach their breeding

In some species, the male not only sings to the female but also displays to her at the same time.

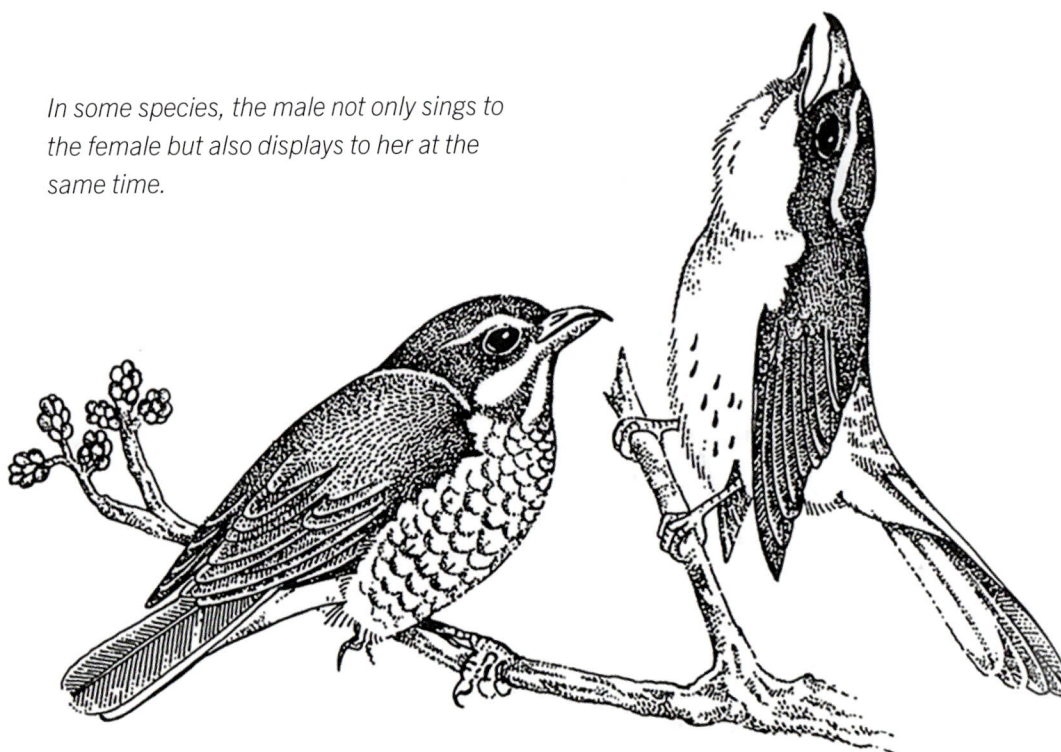

grounds, they will be in full song, ready to establish a territory and find a mate.

Prompted by Daylight

Lengthening daylight hours encourage resident birds to sing; as the days get longer their singing becomes more pronounced and continues for longer periods. Wintering birds are often silent for the whole of their stay south, but occasionally some departing late may be stimulated into song by a particularly springlike day. Birds can be fooled by light levels. In addition, some will begin to sing in fall when the daylight length matches that of spring. This singing soon stops as the days get shorter, however.

In most species, song is at its fullest at the start of breeding, with males singing throughout the day. It wanes slightly during courtship and mating, and picks up again during the incubation period, although males that help with the incubation will sing less. As soon as the eggs hatch and help is needed to feed the young, the male will sing less often, concentrating his territorial song on the area around the nest.

Many birds go silent and molt when their young fledge and need no more attention. Others may have a second brood; if so, the male will sing again with renewed ardor, often re-establishing territorial boundaries. In late summer or fall the hormonal drive tails off, and many birds stop singing altogether, though this pattern of song is a generalization, and there are some species that do not conform. The mockingbird and the cardinal, for instance, sing in every season as they defend their territories throughout the year, while the brown thrasher ceases singing immediately after mating.

Red-wing blackbirds sound out from the singing perches at dawn and dusk, and forage for food at midday.

As well as this annual variation in song, there is also a daily rhythm. Birds that are active during the day will begin singing just before sunrise as the increasing light reaches a certain intensity. As the morning progresses, birds begin to quiet down; singing picks up in the late afternoon, continuing until nearly dusk.

Different species are triggered into song by varying amounts of light, and when listening to a dawn chorus, separate species can be noted as they start. The order in which birds first sing is fairly constant, though it depends upon the birds present. If they are in the vicinity, robins are usually the first to pipe up. In eastern states, the next to sing might be a wood thrush and then a Carolina wren, while out West it would most likely be a hermit thrush and then a Bewick's wren. Chickadees, phoebes, towhees, and sparrows also start singing early.

It is interesting to note that thrushes are commonly found to be the first singers in most countries. In Europe, the blackbird is often first, followed by the song thrush. In India, one of the first is the Indian robin; in southern Africa, it is the kurrichane and olive thrushes. In New Zealand, with its high number of introduced European birds, it is once again the blackbird and the song thrush that begin the chorus.

The contrast between the dawn chorus and the quiet of midday is truly astonishing when you realize the birds are still wide awake, though once again there are exceptions, as certain birds sing consistently throughout the day. Field sparrows, indigo buntings, red-eyed vireos, and prairie warblers are just a few examples. Actually, the red-eyed vireo holds the world record for the number of songs given in a day — a total of 22,197!

Nighttime vocalists

Night is not solely reserved for owls — it is often surprising just what else can be heard under the cover of darkness on a spring night. Mockingbirds are the North American equivalent of the legendary nightingale and can be heard regularly at night, together with yellow-breasted chats. Outbursts of "ecstasy" singing from yellowthroats and ovenbirds add to the night chorus that, of course, also includes species such as whippoorwills.

The dawn chorus can be overwhelming with birdsong. Here an eastern meadowlark adds its song.

Some species enhance their vocal ability with elaborate displays. Early literature often depicts the displays of species such as lyrebirds (top), redstarts (bottom left), and birds of paradise (bottom right).

Where Birds Sing

As the main purpose of song is to deter competitors and attract a mate, it follows that the further a song carries, the better. For this reason, many male singers will choose a prominent perch, such as the top of a tall tree, bush, or rock, and sometimes an artificial song post at the top of a telephone pole or tall building. The song post may be positioned at the edge of a territory, whose boundaries are often marked by a number of these song posts. The actual nest is normally sited well within the territory and, especially with large territories, the male will sing from a perch well away from the nest so as not to attract predators directly to it.

For bird watchers, the fact that different singing birds choose different but consistent perching places helps to locate the bird. This is particularly true of many woodland species, especially warblers. When spring migration is in full swing, a piece of woodland can contain dozens of different species, and it helps enormously that black-throated blue warblers sing from the undergrowth, black-throated green warblers from a middle height, and Cape May warblers from the very top. These levels are also the birds' usual feeding points, so they can be looked for with a greater chance of success even when silent. However, singing, feeding, and nesting levels are not always the same; many thrushes that feed on the ground, for instance, will nest off the ground and sing from the top of a tree. Also, in open areas such as fields, prairie, tundra, and desert, many birds deliver their songs during flight. Larks, longspurs, and pipits will "perch" in the air to deliver their songs.

Birds that sing from exposed perches

The tree pipit delivers its song while floating down to the ground with its wings outstretched.

tend to have shorter song phrases, possibly to reduce the chance of a predator catching them unawares in midsong. Certainly some of the longest songs come from species that stay well hidden, such as the grasshopper warbler, which has a trilling song lasting for more than two minutes. The possible extra vulnerability means that normally song perches are positioned where the singer can see a predator coming, and also near to cover for escape. When birds are establishing song posts, they often try out a few, eventually settling for the safest one that lets them communicate to the widest audience.

A male rufous-sided towhee announces his territory from a singing perch.

Identifying Songbirds

To the inexperienced bird watcher, the way in which a practiced ear can pick out and identify bird sounds seems almost supernatural. Most beginners cannot imagine ever mastering the different sounds, but with practice, it becomes relatively easy. Most people aware of birds will recognize the songs of many birds around them. Learning to recognize the commoner species provides a basis from which to expand. Having learned the songs and calls of birds in your backyard, visit a woodland where many of these familiar birds will be present. Whenever possible, go out with a more experienced bird watcher who will be able to draw your attention to the similarities and differences of songs. An additional help may be a recording, so that it can be played again and again, thereby familiarizing yourself with the birdsongs.

Translating birdsong

Some birdsongs are easier to remember than others, since they lend themselves to verbal descriptions. If you aren't able to record the birdsong, it is useful to familiarize yourself with a means of writing down songs and calls, as this may help to identify them later. Written descriptions are possibly the best way to do this, though what you hear and write down may not correspond with what is written in a book. It is worth practicing by writing out songs from a recording and comparing them with the book.

Recording and Viewing

Many bird enthusiasts take up bird sound recording. To get the best results, specialized and often expensive equipment is needed. Nowadays, large tape recorders of the past have all but vanished and portable cassette recorders and light,

hand-held microphones can produce high-quality recordings. With present-day technology, it is also possible to use your smart phone. If you buy cheaply, the results are likely to be poor, so it's always worth investing in quality equipment. There is such a wide choice of microphones and recorder, plus a bewildering number of terms to contend with, that the best way to choose is to seek advice first from a bird watcher who already records sounds.

For viewing, the barest of essentials are binoculars and a good field guide. On the market today, there is an overwhelming selection of binoculars. Which one you end up with is often dictated by your budget — but a few things should be considered. The very expensive models are optically perfect for viewing under a wide range of conditions. Grinding of the glass allows for maximum use of light under all conditions. They are usually waterproof and dustproof. The prisms of the expensive models are anchored in place much better, and this prevents slippage in heat or when jarred and thereby prevents knocking the binoculars out of alignment. When you pay a lower price, many of these features are lost. In addition, the more expensive glasses can focus extremely close, a feature that is a must for tropical or dense thicket birding. However, for $250 or so, a good pair of binoculars can be had that will fit the average birder's needs. As for power, ask three people and you might get three answers. The standard, and a good choice, is 7 x 35 or 8 x 42 with center and right eye focus. Seven or eight power will allow a very wide depth of field and eliminate the need to keep focusing and refocusing.

Do not be fooled into "the more power, the better I'll see the bird" syndrome. People afield with 15 and 20 power binoculars will find them worthless.

Take the time and look through the binoculars you will purchase; they need to be right to make birding fully enjoyable.

Out in the Field

Familiarity with songbirds is gained by many hours afield; hearing unfamiliar calls, tracking the birds down, and then studying the individual as it sings. As this is being done, many other fragments that will lead to birding competence are being collected. You will begin to understand habitat preference, activity hours for a specific species, preferred levels of activity within the forest for feeding and singing, time of the year when the bird is most active, and perhaps information on the bird's food preference.

One of the best ways to learn about birds is to go out with groups and learn from the experts.

Calls and Postures

Bird calls have different functions from song. Song is used, primarily by male birds, to warn other males to keep away or to attract females. Females of some species, such as the Northern Cardinal in North America, sometimes sing to defend a territory against other females, but their song is more muted than that of males. Calls, on the other hand, are used by birds of all ages and both sexes.

Some calls are simply used to keep in touch, while others give particular messages, even to birds of other species. Certain postures and actions function in a similar way.

Contact calls

A flock of small birds moving through the woods during the winter keeps more or less together in order to maintain vigilance against predators and to improve the chances that one member of the flock will find food that all can exploit. Birds within the flock keep in touch by rather quiet, simple, short call notes, called contact calls.

Such calls often have a long vowel sound but, to our ears, no obvious consonants—they do not have "hard" endings or "shapes" to the sound, and they can often be written down as

"eeee" or "sseee." Similar notes, but with a greater intensity and a sharp or metallic quality, give warning of a predator. These calls are often above the frequency range that is easily heard by a large hawk or falcon, but well within the hearing of small songbirds.

Identifying calls

The lack of a hard edge to call notes also makes them exceedingly difficult to locate. Bird-watchers often hear calls but find it hard to locate the bird that is making the sounds. This allows a small bird to warn others that a predator is near without putting itself at risk. House sparrows use different calls to indicate aerial threats and ground-based threats, such as a cat. If you become familiar with the alarm notes of different birds, you may find that you can recognize the call a bird makes to identify the presence of a hawk, and may improve your chances of seeing these birds of prey.

MOORHENS

The splash of white beneath the tail is used as a means of communication between mates and also between rivals.

ACTING UP

A "broken wing" display is designed to lure predators in pursuit of easy prey away from eggs or chicks.

Warning calls

Adult birds use particular warning calls for their chicks, too. "Keep still" is the obvious meaning of a call when danger approaches. Young birds make long, loud, whining, or squealing notes when they are hungry. One theory to explain such behavior is that it "blackmails" the parents into feeding their chicks to keep them quiet, otherwise, the sounds would attract predators and weeks of effort spent rearing the young would be wasted. An extreme example of this is the young cuckoo, which is reared by foster parents and has a kind of "super" food-begging call. It is so effective that even passing birds that have nothing to do with the cuckoo will stop to feed it. Its loud, wheezing, begging note seems to be an irresistible stimulus.

Small birds make loud alarm calls when they discover a predator, such as an owl roosting in a tree by day. They risk great danger in drawing attention to the owl by "mobbing" it, bringing in a crowd of birds of several species that join in the hue and cry. This may be to make sure that all birds in the area know that the owl is there, or it may help to drive the owl away, or it may even teach young birds that owls are dangerous. Another theory is that such a noise attracts even bigger creatures—such as people—that scare the owl away when they come to investigate.

Postures

A good example of a posture is the injury-feigning of birds such as plovers and skuas. If a predator such as a cat or fox threatens the nest or young, the parent will flutter along the ground, luring the predator away by pretending to be injured and unable to fly. The potential predator misses a meal when the adult judges its young to be safe, suddenly "recovers" and flies away.

Eggs

Birds lay eggs and incubate them externally, in nearly all cases by applying heat from their bodies, until the young bird breaks free. Some small songbird eggs hatch in fewer than 10 days, but the eggs of some species, particularly many seabirds, may require 50 days or more. Albatross eggs, for example, take as long as 80 days to hatch.

Bird eggs contain a developing embryo and various components that nourish and protect it—the yolk, egg white (or albumen), and an air cell. These elements are encased in a more or less smooth, thin, rigid calcium shell of surprising strength that keeps out water, but allows in air. Eggs may be almost round, symmetrically oval or, most often, broader at one end than the other. The narrow end of an egg may be blunt or rather pointed, as in the case of some ground-nesting birds like the Killdeer in North America, which lay four eggs and arrange them neatly, with the pointed ends directed inwards.

Egg design

As the egg is formed, colors and patterns that are characteristic of the species may be laid down on the shell. These sometimes help to camouflage the egg when it is left uncovered in the nest. Hole-nesting birds, including owls and woodpeckers, lay white eggs, which are more easily seen in poor light.

The patterns of an egg are not simply a superficial coloring on the outside of the egg: some markings, such as dark spots and blotches, often concentrated toward the broader end of the egg, are integral parts of the shell's structure. The extra pigment in these blotches strengthens weak areas in the thinnest parts of the shell and they may have other functions as yet unknown.

Eggs are incubated by one or both parents.

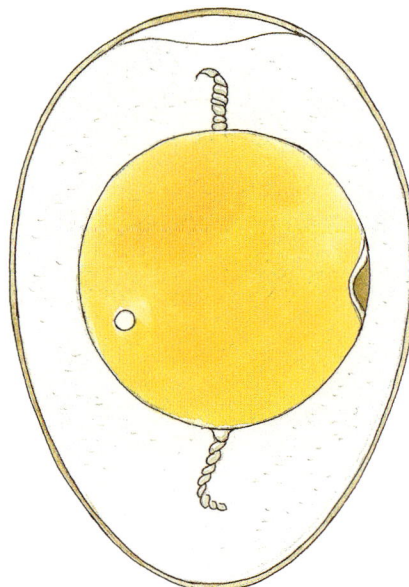

PARTS OF AN EGG

The egg yolk is held in place within the white, or albumen; at the broad end of the egg is an air cell.

An adult bird sits on the eggs to warm them until they hatch, usually with the aid of an "incubation patch"—bare skin on the belly of the incubating bird with no feathers but expanded blood vessels to supply extra heat. The developing chick receives nutrients from the yolk inside the egg and eventually breaks through the shell, using a tiny "tooth" at the tip of its bill.

Chicks can be described as either nidicolous (altricial) or nidifugous (precocial). Nidicolous chicks are weak, more or less naked, and blind,

NIDICOLOUS CHICK

Many chicks hatch out tiny, blind, and naked and then develop within the nest for several days.

NIDIFUGOUS CHICK

Some chicks hatch with a downy coat, strong legs, and good vision and leave the nest within hours.

and they remain in the nest, needing care and shelter until they grow a covering of feathers and are ready to fly. Nidifugous chicks are covered in warm down, are bright-eyed and active, leave the nest within a matter of hours, and immediately find their own food.

Most songbirds are nidicolous, while most terns, sandpipers, plovers, and chicken-like birds are nidifugous. Many species have chicks that are somewhat intermediate to these. The nestlings of hawks, owls, and herons, for example, are downy and more developed at

hatching than those of most songbirds. They are somewhat active when hatched and soon move about onto branches of their nest tree. Some, such as gull chicks, leave the nest in a downy covering, but require more care and feeding than typical nidifugous chicks.

All chicks need to be cared for to some extent, and they are brooded by a parent when they are cold and wet—the brooding adult typically calls the chicks, which nestle among the adult breast and belly feathers or under a drooped wing for warmth and protection.

HOW MANY EGGS?

A full set of eggs is called a clutch. Some long-lived birds that have a long period of immaturity, such as fulmars, lay a single egg each year. Small songbirds may lay one clutch of 10 to 12 eggs, their hatching coinciding with the peak availability of suitable food. Others produce two, three, or even four clutches of 3 to 5 eggs each during a season. Gamebirds, such as quail and pheasants, have only one clutch each year, but may lay up to 15 eggs; sometimes eggs are laid in the same nest by more than one female.

Rearing a Family

Having put so much effort into finding and defending a territory, finding a mate, building a nest, and producing eggs, a parent bird must ensure that its young survive and thrive. To do so, it must defend them from predators, shelter them from hot sun, cold wind, or rain, and keep them well fed.

Chicks on the ground, such as those of plovers, seem extremely vulnerable, but they can scatter when danger threatens. Plover chicks also have excellent camouflage and quickly learn to "freeze," crouching stock still until a parent calls to say that danger has passed. In many ways, songbird chicks in a nest are more vulnerable. The nest may be well hidden and provide shelter, but the chicks are unable to move. Once they are found, there is no escape.

Defending the young
Even small birds fight against hawks, cats, and foxes as best they can. Birds as diverse as swallows, mockingbirds, terns, hawks, and owls may dive at the head of a person who comes too close to a nest containing chicks. Other birds, such as many sparrows, discreetly leave their nest when danger threatens: it is better for the parent to survive than to stay to face a human intruder and risk death, and the nest is less likely to be found if the parent bird is absent.

Even doves, particularly unsuited to aggressive attacks, have been seen diving at a small hawk that has caught a chick. Skuas are much more dynamic, aggressive birds, and they will dive at the head of a person near their breeding area, sometimes striking them. Female harriers, and much smaller Arctic Terns, practice similar behavior.

Feeding the family
Small birds such as tits visit the nest hundreds of times each day to bring food for a growing family. Chicks require a constant supply of energy and need brooding in bad weather—the parent shelters them under its wings and fluffed-out body feathers. Swifts feed their young on flying insects—not as reliable a food source as caterpillars and insects found on foliage. If the weather is wet and windy, the swifts may find it difficult to find food. At such times their chicks become temporarily torpid (they lower their body temperature and become inactive, thus conserving energy)—but swifts may fly hundreds of miles to avoid bad weather, or to exploit insects concentrated along weather fronts. They are among the finest meteorologists in the bird world.

In several species—as varied as Common Moorhens, Long-tailed Tits, Florida Scrub Jays, and Red-cockaded Woodpeckers—parent birds receive help to feed their young from other birds. In Common Moorhens, the young from an early brood help to feed chicks of a later brood. In Long-tailed Tits, helpers are usually brothers of the male parent, with no chicks of their own. In Florida Scrub Jays and Red-cockaded Woodpeckers, the helpers are usually offspring from previous years.

FEEDING CHICKS

Tiny chicks call loudly as long as they are hungry. This forces the parents to either keep feeding them or risk losing the results of weeks of intensive effort.

ENVIRONMENTAL EFFECTS

Some seabirds have struggled in recent years to find food for their chicks. Rising sea temperatures have affected the distribution and abundance of plankton, which are eaten by sand eels, the favored prey of some seabirds. Kittiwakes, terns, and guillemots have been seen catching dozens of tough, leathery pipefish, which have replaced the sand eels in some areas, and trying to feed them to their chicks. The chicks starve, surrounded by uneaten fish, which they are unable to swallow—many choke to death in the attempt. Global warming is also affecting the migratory patterns of some songbirds, which are returning earlier to their breeding grounds. In some cases, the young of these birds are hatching before the insects the parents need to gather for them are emerging, with catastrophic results. Nesting efforts fail for lack of food, and when subsequent insect emergence peaks, it remains uncontrolled by the lowered bird population.

CHAPTER TWO

MAKING THE MOST OF BIRDING

This chapter contains expert tips, techniques, and advice on how best to observe birds: where, when, and what to look for, basic identification, taking notes, making sketches, and using binoculars. This section also teaches you more about the habitats and places you could venture to see more birds, as well information on transforming your backyard into a bird reserve.

Telling Birds Apart

Each species of bird is identifiably different in some way from other bird species. In many cases, the differences are obvious, but in others they are less so and may come down to extremely subtle variations in color, shape, or even the sounds a bird makes. The difficulty of identifying birds therefore varies from easy-for-beginners to challenging—even for specialists.

Beginners to bird-watching should start by identifying common garden and town birds. It is a good idea to get a few basic reference points—the commonest, simplest species—against which other birds can be compared. When you observe a "new" bird you can then think about how it looks compared with the birds you already know. Is it about the size of a sparrow, or as big as a pigeon? Is it the same shape as a robin, or similar to a starling but with a thicker bill? Such basic comparisons are invaluable and your bank of references will grow as you get to know more and more birds. You will then be able to make far more subtle and useful comparisons.

Noting size, shape, and behavior

The size of a bird is one of the first points you should note. This is not always easy, unless the bird is near another species or object with which you are familiar. It can be hard to judge the size of a bird that is flying high in the sky or perched far away across a field, but do your best. Try to get an idea of the bird's basic shape and its bulk. Is it a slim, lightweight, elegant bird, or a big, heavy, lumbering bird? Also take note of the proportions of its body parts in relation to each other. Does it have a large head with a long neck, bill, and legs? Or is the bird round-bodied, short-tailed, and short-legged? Try to get as much of an overall impression as you can when you spot a new or strange bird, including the way it moves and behaves. Is it walking quickly, hopping, or sitting still? Does it dash from bush to bush, or spend many minutes flying around over a field? If the bird is in a bush, does it sit quietly or is it constantly in motion, slipping through the

GO PISH

There are several ways in which you can lure small songbirds to come closer so you can get a better look. "Pishing"—making a repeated, urgent "pshhh pshhh" sound—is one such method. This noise imitates that of a worried bird. Squeaking, with high-pitched squealing and squeaking sounds, also works well. You can also try playing the calls or songs of a bird to force a particular bird to approach to defend his territory against an intruder. This technique can work like magic, but it should be used sparingly and with caution. It tends to be disruptive and can be damaging for the bird. Use the playback technique with great restraint or not at all. Finally, some refuges and sanctuaries forbid the use of recorded calls and their use to lure an endangered species can be illegal.

Scapulars

Secondaries

Primaries

Mantle

Forehead

Eye stripe

Chin

Throat patch

Breast

Belly

Flank

Undertail
coverts

MAKING NOTES

*Try to use the correct terms to describe a
bird in your notes. Some common ones to
use in addition to "head," "eye," or "wing,"
are labeled on the Northern Goshawk
(above) and the European Starling (below).*

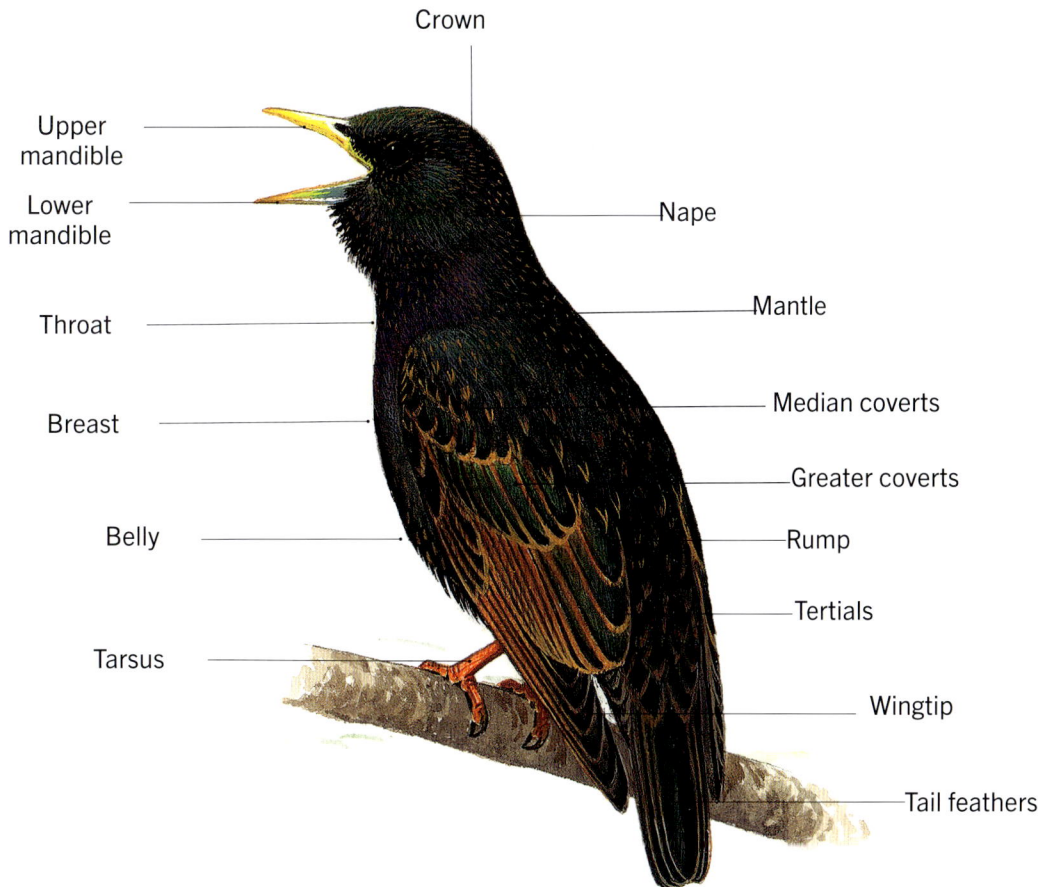

Crown

Upper
mandible

Lower
mandible

Throat

Breast

Belly

Tarsus

Nape

Mantle

Median coverts

Greater coverts

Rump

Tertials

Wingtip

Tail feathers

Pale gray cap

White shoulder patch

Green rump

Large bill

White sides to tail

Pink throat and chin

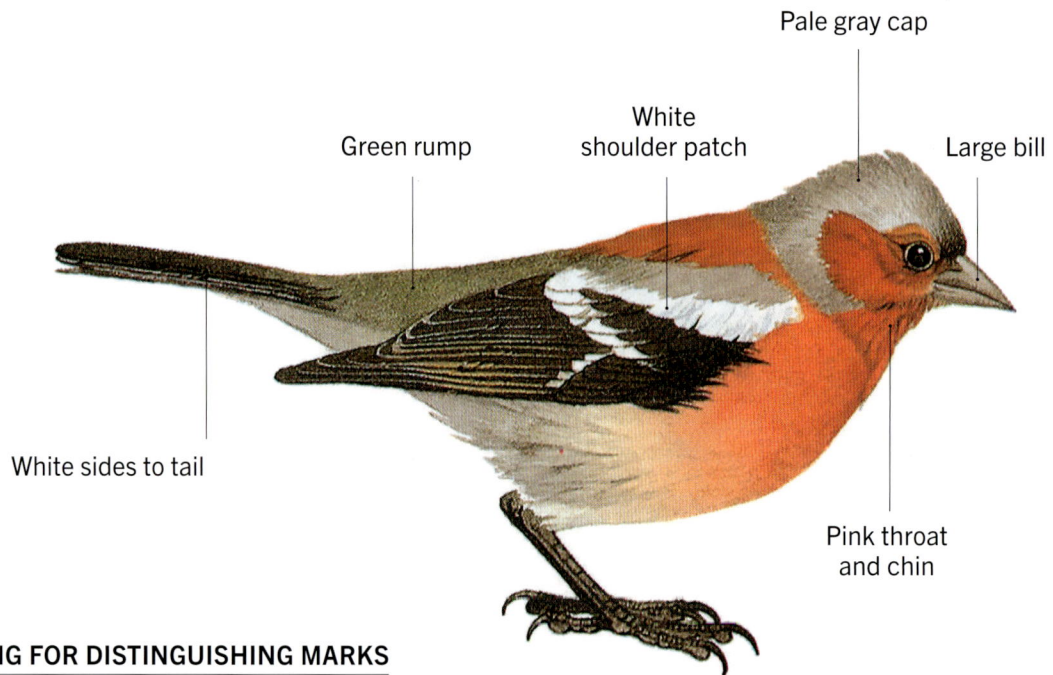

LOOKING FOR DISTINGUISHING MARKS

The bold little Chaffinch may come for crumbs in woodland car parks; its white wing marks are distinctive.

foliage to hop from branch to branch? Does the bird sit and pick its food from the nearest twig or leaf, or does it hang upside down to reach around for its food? Is it alone or is it with other birds of the same or a different species?

Too often bird-watching beginners focus on just one or two points that are immediately obvious—such as a white patch on the body, or a yellow tinge to the wing—and ignore everything else, expecting that this will be enough to make an accurate identification. Usually, they will be disappointed. It is important to get as much information as you can. As you become more experienced, try to use the correct terms to describe the parts of a bird in your notes, including the tracts of feathers such as primaries and wing coverts. This will allow you to be more precise when describing what you have seen, and you will become fluent in the common language of

bird-watchers.

Recognizing old friends

Eventually, the wealth of information you gather will allow you to identify common birds with ease. For example, sparrows feed on the ground and fly away fast and straight to the nearest bush if they are disturbed, while swallows hunt insects in the air and fly in a relaxed, flowing manner, rarely stopping to perch. Thrushes feed on the ground, hopping and running, and stopping to look and listen, or probe the ground with their bill. Goldfinches feed in little groups in the tops of thistles, flitting from flower to flower. Pigeons seem to shuffle along and sit on rooftops for minutes at a time, while kestrels sit on open posts and treetops, coming to the ground only to capture their prey. All of these impressions will soon become familiar and gradually you will be able to recognize what "kind" of bird you are looking at. You can then start to pay closer attention to finer details: observing colors and patterns in plumage and listening to bird sounds. Experienced bird-watchers often do not need these finer details to identify a bird. They will see a bird fly across a field or perch in a bush and be able to name it simply because "that is what it looks like." With some practice, you will be able to do the same.

Identifying birds becomes easier as they become more familiar. It is like spotting a friend on a busy street: you do not have to check the color of the eyes or the shape of the nose, you simply know who it is. However, if you are trying to find someone you have never seen before, and have just a photograph as a reference point, smaller details become more important. Bird-watching works in a similar way. At first you will be looking for all the specific markings of a bird illustrated in a field guide, but eventually you will be able to see the same bird fly by and identify it on sight.

USING YOUR EYES AND EARS

This adult male redpoll has a striking pink breast, but juveniles lack pink, and you need to look carefully for the black chin. Their calls can also help identify them.

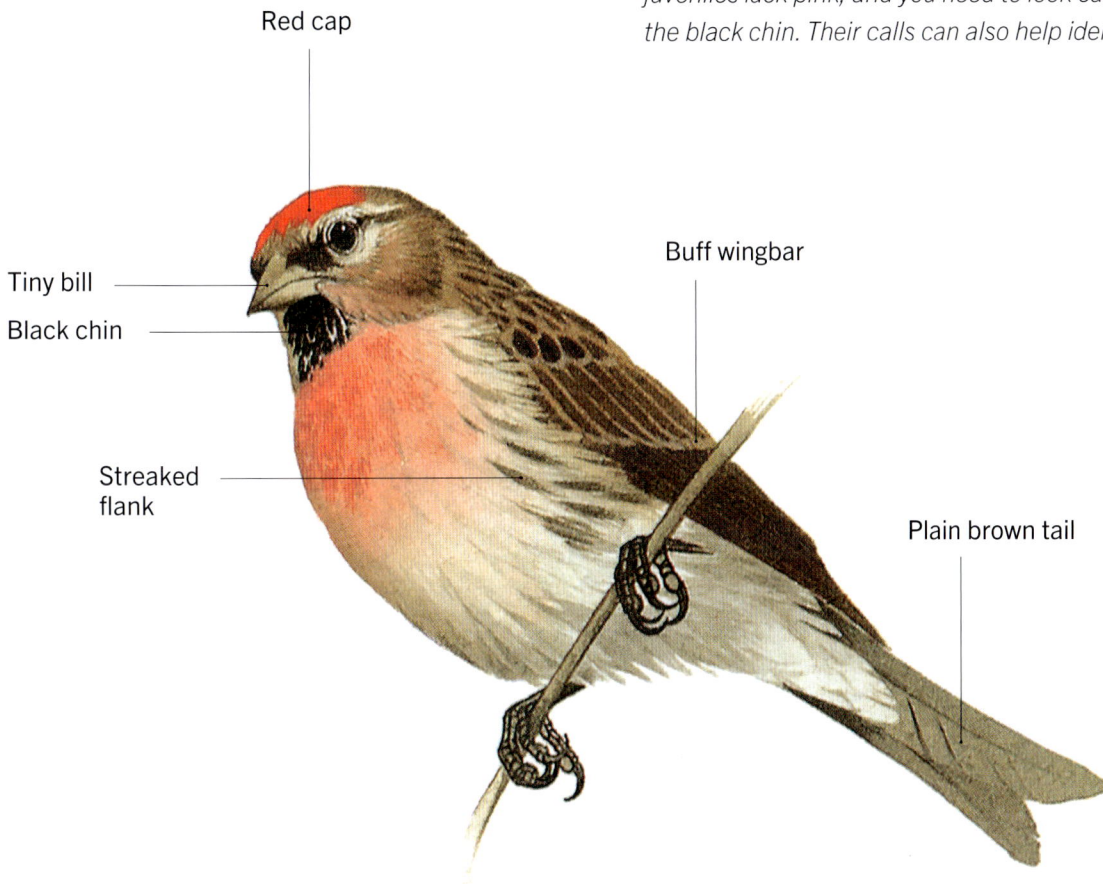

Red cap

Tiny bill

Black chin

Streaked flank

Buff wingbar

Plain brown tail

Taking Notes and Making Sketches

A notebook used to be part of every bird-watcher's outdoor kit. Now most bird-watchers use a digital camera fixed to a telescope to record what they see. Nevertheless, a notebook is exceptionally useful and is an ideal way to remember details about the birds you watch.

If you see something unusual when bird-watching, try to describe it in your notebook as thoroughly as possible. It is difficult to remember everything by memory alone, especially if you want to look up a bird in a book later to identify what you saw. Did the bird have pale brown legs and a buff band on the tail, or did you only read these things in the book? Were there four white spots on the wingtip or just three? It quickly becomes impossible to remember.

Take good notes

If possible, write everything down while you are still watching the bird. You can scribble down your own shorthand and expand on it later. If you get details wrong you can change them as you watch the bird and get a better view. You might write down "black bill" and later change it to "dark brown bill with paler base," or "eyes looked dark" might become "brown eyes with paler ring" once you see the bird more closely.

MALLARD

Even on a common bird like this, the pattern is hard to describe without at least a few specialist terms to pinpoint colors, but they are easy to learn.

Do the best you can, but aim for as detailed an observation as possible.

You never know what crucial feature will help you identify a bird later, so make sure you write everything down. It can be helpful to make a sketch and label all the bird's features. This will make it clear what details are missing—perhaps you haven't labeled the legs, and this will prompt you to get a better look. Making a sketch forces you to look—closely, and properly. You can't draw the right pattern of streaks if you haven't seen them; you're not likely to get the head pattern right if you don't specifically choose to note head-pattern characteristics. Approach bird identification systematically, and know bird anatomy with an awareness of potential patterns of plumage and shapes of head, bill, wings, and tail.

If you are faced with a complicated bird, you can work at studying the details, noting them down, and putting them in a sketch, however crude it might be. Not only will you have to look at the bird carefully to get it right, but you will remember so much more about it, even months later. Taking a bird's picture gives you a quick reference, but fixes little in your mind. A photograph is a record of a tiny moment: it may not be as "true" as you think. How often

SKETCHING A DUCK

Start with a rough idea of shapes and proportions, then add shape, then colors and patterns.

do you take a photograph of someone and find it doesn't really look right—perhaps they moved, or blinked, or turned away at the crucial moment. A photograph of a bird can be just as inaccurate. A drawing, or a written description, made as the bird moves and feeds, flies, and preens, will be a much more complete record than a moment caught by the camera. Of course, you may do both, but don't neglect the old-fashioned notebook and drawing.

How to make a sketch

Even if you are not a skilled artist, any drawing is better than none. Use rough egg shapes to get the basic idea of a head and body—as near as you can get to the right proportions. Is the body elongated horizontally, or vertically? Is it round or thin? Add wings, a tail, legs, and a bill as well as you can. Now put labels on all the features, making short notes with lines pointing to the position on the sketch. Make more sketches as you get a better view of the bird or see it from different angles.

Remember, once you have read a description of a bird, or looked at a photograph or a painting, or listened to a sound track, it is more difficult to remember exactly what you originally saw or heard—details may become obscured. Once you have gone home, you cannot look at the live bird again to check something—so take notes and make sketches while you can. You will not regret it.

Sounds

Bird calls and songs are crucial in helping you to identify a species. Bird-watchers also use them to locate birds, many finding more birds by using their ears than by using their eyes. You can listen to recordings of bird sounds, but learning them directly from the bird that makes them is more effective, as it puts the sound into context and makes it more memorable. The best situation is to see the bird actually making the noise; then you know for certain what noise a species makes and are more likely to remember it later.

You may find it helpful to write down what a bird call sounds like. Use simple words or syllables to describe how the call sounds to you, such as tchew, twit, sweep, or chirrup. Add descriptions of the noise, such as liquid, metallic, sharp, hard, soft, silky, or abrupt. Many bird calls are difficult to describe because they consist of an extended vowel sound without a hard consonant—but do your best.

You can add a clue to the rise and fall and inflection of a call by drawing a line above it. For example, you can use a thick line that tapers out to indicate a call that fades away, or make the line bend up or down to show the rise and fall in pitch of the call. If you need to refer to a book when you get home, these efforts can help you to remember what you heard.

Keeping a diary

Most bird-watchers like to keep some sort of log of the birds they have seen. Those who began bird-watching before personal computers were commonly used probably kept a simple written diary, a card index, or perhaps merely a life-list of birds they have seen. Many people who are starting out today will prefer to keep records on their phone. However, there are pros and cons for every system and none is perfect.

A daily bird-watching diary is useful. Important things to note include the date of the observations, the time, your location, perhaps the weather, and a list of birds you see. You can liven your diary up with the names of your companions, or note the day you first used your new binoculars. A good diary is far more than a basic list of birds—it is also a personal story that can include your thoughts, observations, and excitement at the best (or worst) of times.

In some special circumstances (if, for example, you are keeping detailed reports at a nature reserve), you might note everything you see. Usually, though, this becomes tedious and repetitive, and you will instead be more selective. By neglecting details, however, you risk losing good data on birds that are common now, but might not always be so. There has to be a compromise: keeping notes should add enjoyment to your hobby, not make it a chore, but it should also be useful.

The more you bird-watch, the more you will learn what is worth writing down and what is not. You will, after all, be keeping these notes for yourself, as a rule. They will be private rather than public records. You should send in all the significant and useful notes to a local or county bird recorder, to add to the official record. To do this easily, you may need a system that allows you to find all your notes from one location or all your notes on a particular species. This is where a card index works better than a daily diary. A computer log, on which you can search for specific words, is obviously the most efficient option. While a card index is helpful for finding all your sightings of any one species, it fails to tell you what you saw at a particular place or on a specific day, and it does not bring back memories, or record the atmosphere, in the way that a daily log does. And for many people, a computer diary isn't as "friendly" as a paper one.

THE PROS AND CONS

Do you want to keep the notebooks you take out bird-watching with you? Or do you prefer a more permanent record, written up in an exercise book, or typed onto a computer? You can, of course, keep both, but space becomes a problem over the years. In the end, you will find your own preferred method, but think about what you want from a notebook and try to make it practical—get it to work for you.

	PROS	CONS
Notebook	Portable	Takes up space
	User-friendly	Can be difficult to find information
	Personal and evocative	
Desktop computer	Quick, easy searches	Not portable
	Compact	Cannot use it in the field
	Programs can sort information	
Mobile phone	Quick, easy searches	Impersonal and unevocative
	Compact and portable	Dependent on battery life
	Programs can sort information	

Choosing and Using Binoculars

Apart from a field guide illustrating the area's local birds, the only equipment a bird-watcher needs is a pair of binoculars. A good pair will last a lifetime, so choose carefully and get the best you can afford.

Recommending a particular make and model of binoculars is not easy, because different shapes and sizes suit different people and manufacturers are constantly improving their products and coming out with new ones. For bird-watching, a small, lightweight pair is ideal, but above all, it is important to make sure that binoculars are comfortable to use. They should "fit" your hands and the region around the eyes, so comfort largely depends on personal preference and the size and shape of your hands and face.

Types of binoculars

Binoculars come in two basic types: the roof prism, which looks straight-sided and slim, and

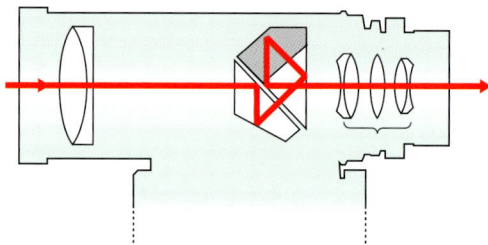

ROOF PRISM

This design is the more modern and efficient type of binoculars.

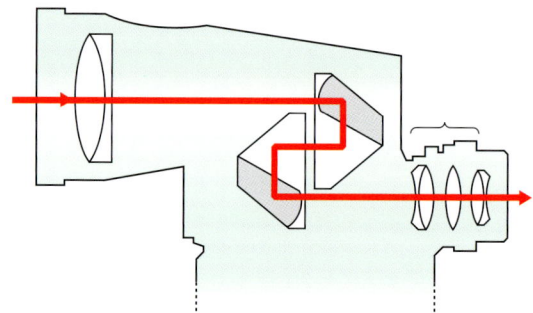

PORRO PRISM

Light is reflected through a prism before reaching the eyepiece.

KEEP THEM CLEAN!

Eyepieces are often smeared with sunscreen, insect repellent, or makeup, and the larger lenses become dirty. Insect repellent can also damage the coating of lenses. When cleaning, avoid rubbing because it damages the lens coating and may grind in dirt, scratching the lens itself. Blow away dirt and dust, then gently brush the lens with a soft cloth designed for lens cleaning. Do not use a shirt or handkerchief, or any tissue paper other than specially made lens paper. It is always best to use a liquid lens cleaner with your lens cloth.

the porro prism, which looks "step-sided" and has much wider front lenses (objective lenses) than eyepieces (ocular lenses). The roof prism is the more efficient system, but you may not notice a difference in the images it magnifies. They are also smaller and lighter in weight, and you can get compact or miniature models, but smaller binoculars let in less light and are less useful in low-light conditions. Try both types at a camera or optics store before making a decision.

One thing to keep in mind: porro prism binoculars have an external focusing mechanism—the front lenses move in and out on a greased rod when the viewer focuses on something. That grease is exposed to dust in the air. Over time, the grease becomes saturated with dust and dirt, making focusing more difficult or even impossible. Roof prism binoculars, on the other hand, have an internal focusing mechanism and therefore do not have any external moving parts that will become gummed up with grease.

Power and lens size

The magnification level (the number of times that an object will be enlarged) and the diameter of the larger lenses (in millimeters) of binoculars is always specified: 10x40 binoculars, for example, magnify the object by 10 times and have 40 mm lenses. For bird-watchers, a magnification, or "power," between 7 and 10 is generally suitable. However, the higher the power, the more difficult it will be to hold them steady—every movement of the hand is magnified as much as the image. You will need a bright image if you are to accurately identify birds. Larger front lenses allow more light in, and the higher the binoculars' power, the larger the lenses need to be to show the magnified picture brightly.

When choosing binoculars, divide the diameter of the front lenses (the second number) by the magnification (the first number) to get the diameter of the "exit pupil"—the bright beam of light that exits the eyepiece. There is no point to having an exit pupil that is larger than the pupil of your eye, as any extra light will be wasted. At its largest, your pupil will be about 7 mm, but in sunlight it is much smaller.

Focusing binoculars

The first adjustment to make takes account of the distance between your eyes, which varies greatly in different people. First, push the barrels closely together. Then point them toward a distant object, raise them to your eyes, and slowly increase the space between the barrels until you see a maximum field of view. This happens when the individual fields of view of the two barrels (the separate images seen by your two eyes) appear to merge and form an oval or circle. The binoculars are now adjusted to fit the distance between your eyes.

Next you must focus the two barrels separately, to take account of the variations in sight between your eyes—even people with good vision usually do not have equally matched sight in both eyes. Once you have made these adjustments, your binoculars are ready to use for observation.

Practice using your binoculars until you can raise them to your eyes without moving your head—this will enable you to keep the bird in sight and avoid disturbing it. Looking directly at the bird (not at the binoculars), raise the binoculars smoothly to your eyes. Swinging your head from side to side with your binoculars in place to get the bird in view is not the way to do it. You can practice this exercise using any object.

Farther Afield

Bird-watching from your window, looking at garden birds, is a good way to start, and garden birds will keep you amused and fascinated for a lifetime. But no doubt you will soon want to explore farther and see different kinds of birds. Your daily routine will reveal only a tiny fraction of the birds out there. Birds are everywhere and you will want to know what species you are looking at.

Look through a field guide and you will see birds you have hardly dreamed of, and they may be close by. If you want to see new birds, the first thing to do is to head for water. Try the beach, a flooded gravel pit, or a reservoir. Water and the water's edge provide habitats for a huge number and variety of birds.

CANADA GOOSE

Even common birds such as the Canada Goose have particular needs and take you away from your backyard—head for water to see this one.

Watching around water

Gravel pits tend to be quite deep and steep-sided, so they are ideal for several kinds of ducks, especially diving ducks such as Ring-necked Ducks, Redheads, and Buffleheads, but not necessarily for those that potter about in the shallows such as Green-winged Teal, and shovelers. Gravel pits often contain grebes and perhaps geese or swans. Reservoirs in steep-sided valleys between high hills tend to be cold, deep, and acidic, and have few birds on the whole. But those created on lowland farmland in wide, shallow valleys can be exceptional. The shores become muddy, and any small drop in water level is likely to reveal vast areas of mud, which becomes overgrown in the summer but flooded again in fall, releasing a superabundance of seeds for winter wildfowl to eat.

The shallow sides attract wading birds on their spring and fall migrations, too. These can be some of the most exciting birds you can find—not only are the common ones beautiful species that may be on their way to the Southern Hemisphere from the Arctic, but the chances of finding something quite rare are fairly good. The water's edge is excellent, too, for birds such as meadowlarks, pipits, finches, and various sparrows. Insects over the water attract early migrants, and flocks of swallows and swifts often gather there in bad weather, when food is hard to find elsewhere. Over the water, too, may be migrant terns, and from late summer to spring, there may well be a big nighttime roost of gulls flying in to find a safe place to sleep after feeding on local farmland or refuse tips.

Any area around these watery places is worth exploring. Willow thickets, bramble and scrub patches, reeds, and rushes are all likely to have interesting breeding birds and migrants that rely on the proximity to water to provide a reliable supply of insects.

On the coast the possibilities are endless. A rocky shore appeals to certain species, while a sandy one may be less rich in birds. But mud, especially in a big estuary, is a super-rich habitat with a fantastic supply of food, which is refreshed twice a day by the tide. As the tide falls, huge numbers of shorebirds of many kinds spread out over the flats. This can be challenging bird-watching, as birds are at long range and conditions are often difficult, but it can be remarkably rewarding. Often, too, there are roads—even urban promenades—that overlook wonderful places for birds in estuarine locations. A trip to the seashore to look for birds should be timed to arrive at low tide.

Other habitats

Woodlands are full of birds, but are often tricky places in which to bird-watch. Dense summer foliage makes things difficult and, in winter, birds are fewer and more concentrated in wandering flocks. It is best to go early in the day in spring, when everything is singing and the leaves are still sparse, or to wander patiently in winter until you come across a mixed flock, when things will suddenly be hectic for a minute or two before they pass by. For birds of prey, it is often best to stay outside the wood, preferably on a hill from

EASTERN MEADOWLARK
Some birds are widespread on farmland, others need old pastures or natural grasslands.

which you can look out across the forest and watch for birds displaying over the forest in spring. Woodpeckers, warblers, thrushes, nuthatches, and creepers are typical woodland birds.

Scrublands are wide-open, sometimes bleak places, and birds can be few and far between except in spring and summer. You need to be patient. Walk slowly and carefully, checking bushes and thickets and looking overhead for passing birds of prey. Their special species make these habitats well worth the visit, but finding all their secrets may take time.

Mountains and hillsides have some special birds, but these are expansive habitats, and you must be sure you are safe—the weather can change dramatically. Take care, wear the right footwear, take food and drink, a map, and warm clothing. But do try to see some mountain birds if you can. It is often possible to do so from a roadside, but you might need to climb a hilltop or explore a valley: keep high and look over the lower areas. The Golden Eagle, Peregrine Falcon, and ptarmigans are highlights to seek out in the mountains.

Make Your Backyard a Bird Reserve

Transforming your yard into a refuge for wildlife is easy to do, is good fun, and brings great rewards. With a little effort, you can attract beautiful songbirds and other interesting wildlife to your yard, which the whole family can enjoy watching. Creating a bird sanctuary can help you unwind and relieve the stress of the working week.

Gardening practices that help wildlife, reduce chemicals in your yard, and conserve water also help to improve the quality of air, water, and soil throughout your neighborhood. Backyards can support wildlife all year round, but birds need your help most during the colder months and in the early spring when wild food is still scarce and winter supplies are already exhausted. Feeding wild birds is a popular hobby, second only to gardening in North America.

A safe environment

Keeping your bird feeders clean is vitally important—unhygienic practices are more likely to lead to disease in the birds that feed in your garden. Placing them in the right place is also necessary if you want to keep birds safe from predators and other dangers (see How to Feed Birds in the Garden, pp. 28–29). Predation by household cats is a major cause of backyard bird deaths, and a study by the American Birding Association found cats to be significant killers of birds that come to feeders. A single domestic household cat can kill more than 100 birds and small mammals each year: even if one bird a month is killed in this way, it still translates to millions of birds being killed by pet cats throughout the U.S. Make sure you place feeders away from anywhere a cat can lie in ambush.

Window strikes are a frequent cause of injury or death to birds—reflections on a big window on a sunny day may create the illusion of an open space that birds may try to fly through. You should take measures to reduce the risk of window strikes. Simply relocating a feeder may help the problem. There are also many ways to disrupt reflections in windows, such as putting stickers on the windows or hanging netting or objects outside them. Shiny objects in particular are more likely to deter birds from approaching.

Making your garden hospitable

What kind of habitat do you have in your own backyard? A pile of brush may be unsightly, but it can help birds escape predators such as cats and Sharp-shinned Hawks. A good thick shrub or hedge can do the same. It should be within easy reach of the feeder, but not so close that a cat can leap out to pounce on a bird.

You should provide birds with water for drinking and bathing. If you do not have room for a pond, a birdbath will suffice, but make sure you keep it topped up with clean, fresh water. A small pond is by far a better option, though, if you are able to create one. It should be quite deep, and lined with old carpet beneath a layer of plastic or rubber pond liner. Also add a layer of earth. Or else you can simply buy an artificial pond. Make sure some of the pond's edges are shallow and slope gradually so that birds can walk in gently: they don't like having to plunge straight in out of their depth. Add a selection of native waterside plants, but leave some open space, too, around the pond edge. It is best not to have fish in a garden pond, as they eat insects and tadpoles. This setup is better suited for a wildlife garden.

As well as setting up a selection of feeders, you should provide other food sources for birds: plants and trees with fruits and berries, or flowers that attract plenty of insects. If you have the space, dead trees or branches help birds such as woodpeckers to find food and nest sites.

If you want to get serious about backyard wildlife, you can register with the Backyard Wildlife Habitat Program with the National Wildlife Federation, which acknowledges the efforts of people who garden for wildlife, gives personal registration certificates, and adds wildlife gardens to the national register of backyard wildlife habitats.

BIRDBATH

Birds need to bathe regularly to keep in good shape, even in cold weather.

DIRECTORY

The pages that follow feature over 100 birds that can be found in the United States. Those that can be seen in and around gardens and towns are examined, along with some that are easy to see up close in locations such as a town park (especially if it has a lake) or in nearby farmland. This directory includes illustrations and details that will help you to identify these species: size, habitat, distribution during the breeding season and during winter, and preferred foods. Two of the species here—House Sparrow and Rock Pigeon—are non-native species that were introduced to North America. Once you go beyond the habitats described here, you will begin to see many more species, and a more comprehensive identification guide will be needed.

INDIGO BUNTING

SIZE: 5 ½ in (14 cm)

HABITAT: Cut-over areas, re-growth burn sites, powerlines, weedy fields, orchards, parks.

RANGE: Eastern half of U.S. with a population extending into southern New Mexico and Arizona.

FOOD: A wide variety of seeds from grasses and other grains to composites.

THE SONG

_ _ ⁄ ⁄

SWEE SWEE-SEET SEET -

⌇ ⌇ ~ ~

SAYA SAYA-SEEO SEEO

NOTE SEQUENCE: A series of paired phrases delivered at a high pitch.

TIME OF SONG: All day.

OTHER BIRDS WITH SIMILAR SONG: Lazuli Bunting (Passerina amoena), but slower and more strident in tone.

YELLOW-BILLED CUCKOO

SIZE: 11 inches (28 cm)

HABITAT: Open woods, orchards, streamside trees.

RANGE: South America.

FOOD: Insects, especially caterpillars.

DOUBLE-CRESTED CORMORANT

SIZE: 27 inches (69 cm)

HABITAT: Rivers, lakes, park lakes, coasts.

RANGE: Pacific coast, Atlantic and Gulf coasts, North Carolina to Belize.

FOOD: Fish.

ROCK PIGEON

SIZE: 11 inches (28 cm)

HABITAT: Towns, cities, quarries, cliffs, farmland, parks.

RANGE: Throughout N America.

FOOD: Seeds and scraps.

MOURNING DOVE

SIZE: 10½ inches (27 cm)

HABITAT: Suburbia, woodland edge, farmland with trees.

RANGE: Throughout N America.

FOOD: Seeds and shoots.

WHITE-THROATED SWIFT

SIZE: 6 ½ in (17 cm)

HABITAT: Mountains and sea cliffs.

RANGE: N Central America and W U.S.

FOOD: Flying insects.

BLACK SWIFT

SIZE: 7 in (18 cm)

HABITAT: Mountains.

RANGE: W North America from Alaska to California and Central America S to Costa Rica, West Indies; winters in tropical America.

FOOD: Insects.

CHIMNEY SWIFT

SIZE: 5 inches (13 cm)

HABITAT: Open air throughout, nesting in hollow trees and chimneys.

RANGE: E North America; winters in South America.

FOOD: Flying insects.

RUBY-THROATED HUMMINGBIRD

SIZE: 3 inches (7½ cm)

HABITAT: Gardens, woodland edges with flowers.

RANGE: Mexico and Central America.

FOOD: Nectar, tiny insects, spiders.

RED-BELLIED WOODPECKER

SIZE: 8½ inches (22 cm)

HABITAT: Woodlands, orchards, gardens, parks.

RANGE: Great Lakes; New England to Gulf states.

FOOD: Insects, seeds, berries.

NORTHERN FLICKER

SIZE: 11 inches (28 cm)

HABITAT: Open forests, farmland with trees, parks, towns.

RANGE: Alaska south through Canada and U.S.

FOOD: Insects, seeds.

RED-HEADED
WOODPECKER

SIZE: 7½ inches (19 cm)

HABITAT: Farms, roadsides, open woodland, towns.

RANGE: Northern birds move south.

FOOD: Insects, fruit, some seeds.

HAIRY WOODPECKER

SIZE: 7½ inches (19 cm)

HABITAT: Woods, parks, orchards, suburbia.

RANGE: Alaska and forested Canada south to western Panama.

FOOD: Insects, berries, seeds, nuts.

TREE SWALLOW

SIZE: 5 inches (13 cm)

HABITAT: Open areas near water, meadows, lakes.

RANGE: Southern U.S. to Central America.

FOOD: Flying insects.

BARN SWALLOW

SIZE: 6 inches (15 cm)

HABITAT: Farms, streamsides, meadows, parks.

RANGE: Most of North America.

FOOD: Flying insects.

PURPLE MARTIN

SIZE: 7 inches (18 cm)

HABITAT: Open country, farms, gardens; breeds in artificial martin houses.

RANGE: Southern Canada to Gulf states; less common in western regions.

FOOD: Flying insects.

BLUE JAY

SIZE: 10 inches (25 cm)

HABITAT: Oak and pine woods, suburbia.

RANGE: Eastern North America from southern Canada to Gulf states.

FOOD: Insects, seeds, nuts, berries, eggs, scraps.

CALIFORNIA SCRUB-JAY

SIZE: 13 inches (33 cm)

HABITAT: Woodlands, chaparral, pastures, backyards.

RANGE: Western U.S. and south to central Mexico.

FOOD: Insects, nuts, seeds, berries, rodents, eggs.

GRAY JAY

SIZE: 11 ½ in (29 cm)

HABITAT: Northern coniferous woods.

RANGE: Boreal forest from Alaska to New-foundland south to Canada and the north of the U.S., as well as in the Rockies and south Cascades.

FOOD: Omnivorous including the young of other birds; makes caches of food; at feeder will take seeds, bread, cracked corn, and suet.

THE SONG

TEELA WOO WHEEOO CHUCK CHUCK

NOTE SEQUENCE: Bubbling, guttural, and warbled notes often delivered on the wing; also a harsh chuck chuck.

TIME OF SONG: All day.

OTHER BIRDS WITH SIMILAR SONG: Steller's Jay and Clark's Nutcracker also "chuckle."

RED-BREASTED NUTHATCH

SIZE: 4 ½ in (11 cm)

HABITAT: Mainly coniferous woods but into mixed woodlands especially during irruption years.

RANGE: Across Canada and the northern portion of the U.S., moving south in the winter.

FOOD: Small insects, their egg cases and larvae, pine seeds, mixed berries.

THE SONG

— — — — — — — —

YANK YANK YANK YANK YANK YANK

NOTE SEQUENCE: A nasal series of rapid notes.

TIME OF SONG: All day.

OTHER BIRDS WITH SIMILAR SONG: The White-breasted Nuthatch (Sitta carolinensis), has a similar but lower, less emphatic call.

WHITE-BREASTED NUTHATCH

SIZE: 5–6 inches (13–15 cm)

HABITAT: Forests, shelter belts, gardens with trees.

RANGE: Southern Canada to Mexico.

FOOD: Nuts, berries, seeds, insects.

HOUSE WREN

SIZE: 4–5 inches (10–13 cm)

HABITAT: Woods, thickets, gardens, parks.

RANGE: Northern birds move into southern parts of range.

FOOD: Insects, spiders, small seeds.

WINTER WREN

SIZE: 3½–4 inches (9–10 cm)

HABITAT: Woods, gardens, parks, thickets.

RANGE: Canada from southeast Alaska, Pacific states, southern half of eastern U.S.

FOOD: Insects, spiders.

CANYON WREN

SIZE: 5 ½ in (14 cm)

HABITAT: Steep-sided canyon faces and rock slides.

RANGE: Western U.S. from central Washington south through California and west Texas to Mexico.

FOOD: All forms of insects, spiders.

THE SONG

TEE — TOO TEW TEW TOO TEW

NOTE SEQUENCE: A loud ringing series of liquid notes which spiral downwards.

TIME OF SONG: All day.

OTHER BIRDS WITH SIMILAR SONG: The single "jeet" note can be similar to the Rock Wren of the same habitat.

CACTUS WREN

SIZE: 8 ½ in (22 cm)

HABITAT: Dry areas with cacti.

RANGE: Southwestern U.S. from southern California to south Texas on into Mexico.

FOOD: Insects, cacti fruit, at feeder attracted by fruits such as half oranges.

THE SONG

CHA CHA CHA RACH CHICK RA RA

NOTE SEQUENCE: Scolding series of harsh notes rising and falling in sequence. Also a rollicking, gurgling call.

TIME OF SONG: All day.

OTHER BIRDS WITH SIMILAR SONG: All species of wrens tend to have harsh, scolding notes.

BEWICK'S WREN

SIZE: 5 ¼ in (13 cm)

HABITAT: Thickets and waste areas, over-grown fields, gardens, chaparral of the West Coast.

RANGE: Western Texas south to Mexico and west to California. North on the coast to Washington with pockets in the southeast.

FOOD: Insects, their egg cases, and larvae; at feeder takes seeds, suet, and fruit.

THE SONG

SEEP SEEP — JEJEJE JEET JEET

NOTE SEQUENCE: A jumbled series of chattering notes starting with clear whistles which sound as if they are inhaled.

TIME OF SONG: All day.

OTHER BIRDS WITH SIMILAR SONG: Similar to House Wren (Troglodytes aedon), but raspy "inhale" note at start distinguishes it.

MARSH WREN

SIZE: 5 in (13 cm)

HABITAT: Fresh and brackish reed and cattail marshes.

RANGE: Across northern half of U.S. and western Canada, coastal California, Nevada and Utah.

FOOD: Small insects and invertebrates, seeds on occasion.

THE SONG

SH-SH-SH

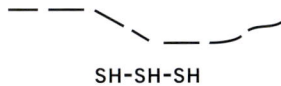

NOTE SEQUENCE: A bubbling series of harsh notes delivered in a rapid rolling pattern; call sh-sh-sh or check-check.

TIME OF SONG: All day.

OTHER BIRDS WITH SIMILAR SONG: Sedge Wren has bubbly, rattling song.

GOLDEN-CROWNED KINGLET

SIZE: 3½ inches (9 cm)

HABITAT: Coniferous woods, gardens.

RANGE: Southward to Gulf states.

FOOD: Insects, spiders.

RUBY-CROWNED KINGLET

SIZE: 4–5 inches (10–13 cm)

HABITAT: Conifers and mixed woodlands.

RANGE: Alaska, Canada, western U.S., extreme northeastern U.S.

FOOD: Insects, spiders.

AMERICAN REDSTART

SIZE: 5 inches (13 cm)

HABITAT: Deciduous woods.

RANGE: Canada and eastern U.S.

FOOD: Insects.

WRENTIT

SIZE: 6 inches (15–16 cm)

HABITAT: Chaparral, confierous brushland, coastal scrub.

RANGE: Central and coastal California, north to coastal Oregon.

FOOD: Insects and berries.

YELLOW-RUMPED WARBLER

SIZE: 5–6 inches (13–15 cm)

HABITAT: Coniferous and mixed woods, thickets.

RANGE: Northeastern U.S., Pacific and Gulf coasts south to Panama.

FOOD: Insects.

AMERICAN ROBIN

SIZE: 9–11 inches (23–28 cm)

HABITAT: Cities, towns, parks, gardens, open woodland, orchards.

RANGE: Across U.S. and Central America.

FOOD: Worms, insects, berries, and fruit.

KENTUCKY WARBLER

SIZE: 5 ¼ in (13 cm)

HABITAT: Boggy woodlands, bushy swamps.

RANGE: Southeastern U.S.

FOOD: Insects and small invertebrates.

THE SONG

— · — — · —

TORY-TORY — TORY- TORY

NOTE SEQUENCE: Loud and rolling. "Hurry hurry hurry" or "tory-tory-tory".

TIME OF SONG: Morning.

OTHER BIRDS WITH SIMILAR SONG: Similar to Carolina Wren found in same area, but lacking any raspy sections.

NORTHERN PARULA WARBLER

SIZE: 4 ½ in (11 cm)

HABITAT: Coniferous forests with Usnea lichen and mixed woods with Spanish moss; on migration, all forest types.

RANGE: Canada to Florida and west to Texas.

FOOD: Insects, eggs, and larvae.

THE SONG

SEE SEE SEE SEE SE ZIP BZZZIP

NOTE SEQUENCE: Series of short buzzy notes that rise up the scale rapidly and end with bzzzip.

TIME OF SONG: Morning.

OTHER BIRDS WITH SIMILAR SONG: The closest similar call is the Cerulean Warbler, which is more hurried at the end.

YELLOW WARBLER

SIZE: 5 in (13 cm)

HABITAT: Wet areas, especially with willows; open woodland, parkland.

RANGE: Across Canada and throughout the northern two-thirds of the U.S.

FOOD: Mainly insects, some spiders, and other small invertebrates.

THE SONG

— — — ⌃ —

SWEET SWEET SWEET OH SO SWEET

NOTE SEQUENCE: Very rapid and pure in quality.

TIME OF SONG: All day.

OTHER BIRDS WITH SIMILAR SONG: In spring, the sweet song of the American Goldfinch (Carduelis tristis), is similar but longer in duration.

CHESTNUT-SIDED WARBLER

SIZE: 5 in (13 cm)

HABITAT: Areas of secondary growth, shrubbery, thickets, overgrown meadows, fields, powerlines.

RANGE: Across southeastern Canada and north central and northeastern U.S.

FOOD: Insects, including defoliating caterpillars, spiders; in winter some seeds and berries.

THE SONG

PLEASE-PLEASE-PLEASE TA MEET CHA

NOTE SEQUENCE: A series of distinct phrases delivered in rapid sequence.

TIME OF SONG: All day.

OTHER BIRDS WITH SIMILAR SONG: Somewhat similar to Yellow Warbler (Dendroica petechia), but more distinct in phrasing.

BLACK-THROATED BLUE WARBLER

SIZE: 5 ¼ in (13 cm)

HABITAT: Mixed woodland with understory.

RANGE: Eastern half of North America and south through the Appalachians.

FOOD: Small insects, grubs and larvae, and spiders.

THE SONG

_ _ _ ⁄

I'M SO LAZY

NOTE SEQUENCE: Of a buzzy, wheezy quality, distinct at first then rapidly rising up the scale.

TIME OF SONG: Morning and midday.

OTHER BIRDS WITH SIMILAR SONG: Similar to an American Redstart (Setophaga ruticilla), but slower and more emphatic at the end.

PINE WARBLER

SIZE: 5 ½ in (14 cm)

HABITAT: Pine woodlands, mixed woodland on migration.

RANGE: Eastern half of North America.

FOOD: Insects, pine seeds, and some berries.

THE SONG

— — — — —

CHEE CHEE CHEE CHEE CHEE

NOTE SEQUENCE: A continuous musical trill of chip notes.

TIME OF SONG: All day.

OTHER BIRDS WITH SIMILAR SONG: Similar to a Chipping Sparrow (Spizella passerina), but not as raspy.

BLACKPOLL WARBLER

SIZE: 5 ½ in (14 cm)

HABITAT: Coniferous forests during breeding season, mixed forests during migration.

RANGE: Alaska across Canada to northern New England.

FOOD: Various small, winged insects, larval forms and egg cases, spiders.

THE SONG

— - - - - - — - - - -

TSEE — SEE-SEE-SEE SEE-SEE

NOTE SEQUENCE: High-pitched and penetrating.

TIME OF SONG: All day.

OTHER BIRDS WITH SIMILAR SONG: The Bay-breasted Warbler has a series of high-pitched notes but they are grouped in double series.

BLACK-AND-WHITE WARBLER

SIZE: 5 ¼ in (13 cm)

HABITAT: Open deciduous and mixed woodlands, swamplands. On migration turns up in parks and gardens.

RANGE: Eastern half of North America.

FOOD: Insects, their eggs, larvae, pupae, and spiders gleaned from trunk and limb surfaces.

THE SONG

WEE-SEE WEE-SEE WEE-SEE

NOTE SEQUENCE: A pulsating series of high lisping notes with greatest inflection on the first part of song.

TIME OF SONG: Morning and night.

OTHER BIRDS WITH SIMILAR SONG: Similar to a Common Yellowthroat (Geothlypis trichas), but much higher pitched and reedy.

WILSON'S WARBLER

SIZE: 4 ¾ in (12 cm)

HABITAT: Thickets and scrub on migration, any area with dense cover.

RANGE: Across Canada and from Alaska south in the Rockies and Cascades.

FOOD: Small insects.

THE SONG

CHEE CHEE CHEE CHET CHET

NOTE SEQUENCE: A wispy, high-pitched and rapid series, dropping off rapidly at the end of sequence.

TIME OF SONG: All day.

OTHER BIRDS WITH SIMILAR SONG: Similar to Canada Warbler but more hurried and less complex.

PROTHONOTARY WARBLER

SIZE: 5 ½ in (14 cm)

HABITAT: Swamps, wet lowlands, bayous.

RANGE: Central and southeastern U.S.

FOOD: Small insects.

THE SONG

— — — —

SWEET-WEET-WEET-WEET-WEET

NOTE SEQUENCE: A sweet series of notes maintained at the same pitch.

TIME OF SONG: Morning.

OTHER BIRDS WITH SIMILAR SONG: Somewhat like a Yellow Warbler (Dendroica petechia), but not as jumbled at the end.

CONNECTICUT WARBLER

SIZE: 5 ¾ in (14 cm)

HABITAT: Cold northern tamarack swamps.

RANGE: Southern, central Canada to north Great Lakes region.

FOOD: Insects.

THE SONG

— — — —

SEE TO IT SEE TO IT

NOTE SEQUENCE: A loud ringing series rising in volume.

TIME OF SONG: Morning.

OTHER BIRDS WITH SIMILAR SONG: Similar to Ovenbird (Seiurus aurocapillus), which does not occur in the same breeding area.

GREAT-CRESTED FLYCATCHER

SIZE: 8 ½ in (22 cm)

HABITAT: Woods and orchards.

RANGE: Eastern half of the U.S. from the Dakotas to New England south to Texas and Florida.

FOOD: Insects.

THE SONG

WEEERRRRUP WEEERRRRUP TREERT

NOTE SEQUENCE: A rising inflection weerrup or a loud echoing treert, sounding similar to a whistle being blown.

TIME OF SONG: Morning.

OTHER BIRDS WITH SIMILAR SONG: Most of the Myiarchus Flycatchers have rolling, rough calls.

OLIVE-SIDED FLYCATCHER

SIZE: 7 ½ in (19 cm)

HABITAT: Dead trees in coniferous forest, especially spruce in north of range and pitch pine in the south.

RANGE: Across Canada and south Alaska and in the mountains to California, Arizona and northern New England.

FOOD: Insects.

THE SONG

QUICK, THREE-BEERS

NOTE SEQUENCE: A distinct three-parted series; the phrase is drawn out.

TIME OF SONG: All day.

OTHER BIRDS WITH SIMILAR SONG: The whip, whip note sounds similar to the Great-crested Flycatcher (Myiarchus crinitus).

VERMILLION FLYCATCHER

SIZE: 6 in (15 cm)

HABITAT: The scrub and trees that fringe watercourses in arid areas.

RANGE: Southern portion of Arizona, New Mexico and Texas; strays to California and east to Florida in winter.

FOOD: Insects.

THE SONG

_-⁄ _-⁄ _-⁄

HIT-A-SEE HIT-A-SEE

NOTE SEQUENCE: A series of rather explosive notes in sequence with rising inflection on the last portion of the three-parted song.

TIME OF SONG: Morning and evening.

OTHER BIRDS WITH SIMILAR SONG: Similar to song of Say's Phoebe (Sayornis saya).

WILLOW FLYCATCHER

SIZE: 5 ½ in (14 cm)

HABITAT: Wet meadows and field edges.

RANGE: New England to south Appalachians, west to northwest to southwest. Avoids the Great Plains.

FOOD: Insects.

THE SONG

FITZ-BEW FITZ-BEW FITZ-BEW

NOTE SEQUENCE: Snappy and two-parted, it ends with a wispy quality.

TIME OF SONG: All day.

OTHER BIRDS WITH SIMILAR SONG: Other Empidonax Flycatchers have wheezy songs but their diagnostic phrasing separates the species.

LOGGERHEAD SHRIKE

SIZE: 9 inches (23 cm)

HABITAT: Shrubs, farmland, desert, fields, parks.

RANGE: Southern, west central, and western U.S.

FOOD: Insects, birds and small mammals.

CEDAR WAXWING

SIZE: 6 inches (15 cm)

HABITAT: Woodland, orchards, parks, gardens.

RANGE: From southern Canada south to Panama.

FOOD: Insects, berries.

EUROPEAN STARLING

SIZE: 8 inches (20 cm)

HABITAT: Cities, parks, farms, gardens.

RANGE: Across U.S., northern birds move south.

FOOD: Insects, worms, fruit, berries, seeds.

BACHMAN'S SPARROW

SIZE: 6 in (15 cm)

HABITAT: Pinewoods and brush In North.

RANGE: Southern U.S.

FOOD: Mainly small seeds.

THE SONG

TOOLY TERE TA SEE TA SA TOO LEE

NOTE SEQUENCE: A lovely rolling flute-like series of two-parted notes with rising, then falling inflection.

TIME OF SONG: Morning and evening.

OTHER BIRDS WITH SIMILAR SONG: Hermit Thrush (Catharus guttatus).

TREE SPARROW

SIZE: 6 in (15 cm)

HABITAT: In summer, scrubby tundra north of the tree line; in winter, weedy patches, marsh edges, and brush piles.

RANGE: Alaska and northern Canada, winter across upper U.S.

FOOD: On breeding grounds mainly insects and seeds.

THE SONG

SEE SEE — TA TEEDLE EE TEA TRAY

NOTE SEQUENCE: A sweet-noted introduction, followed by a fast run of notes ending in a lower pitch.

TIME OF SONG: All day.

OTHER BIRDS WITH SIMILAR SONG: Somewhat like liquid notes of Fox Sparrow (Passerella iliaca).

CHIPPING SPARROW

SIZE: 5 ½ in (14 cm)

HABITAT: Open areas of all types — lawns, parks, farmland, prairie.

RANGE: Across Canada and the U.S.

FOOD: Small seeds of grasses and weeds, insects, spiders, and other invertebrates.

THE SONG

– – – — – –

CHIP-CHIP-CHIP-CHIP-CHIP

NOTE SEQUENCE: A staccato series of high-pitched chips, uttered more in early morning and afternoon.

TIME OF SONG: All day.

OTHER BIRDS WITH SIMILAR SONG: Like a Pine Warbler (Dendroica pinus), but more staccato.

HENSLOW'S SPARROW

SIZE: 5 in (12 cm)

HABITAT: Wet scrubby fields, old meadows, salt marshes.

RANGE: Northeast and central states.

FOOD: Seeds and small insects.

THE SONG

TIS-LICK

NOTE SEQUENCE: A short, sharp double note with rising inflection.

TIME OF SONG: From dusk through the night.

OTHER BIRDS WITH SIMILAR SONG: Unlike any other bird's song. More like a cricket's chirp.

VESPER SPARROW

SIZE: 6 in (15 cm)

HABITAT: Open areas — grasslands, sand and gravel pits.

RANGE: Across northern North America.

FOOD: Grass seeds, berries.

THE SONG

TEAR-TEAR TORE-TORE-HERE-WE-GO-

DOWN-THE-HILL

NOTE SEQUENCE: A progression of two phrase sequences that scale downward in rapid succession.

TIME OF SONG: Morning and evening.

OTHER BIRDS WITH SIMILAR SONG: Similar to a Lincoln's Sparrow, which has a sweet, bubbly trill.

WHITE-THROATED SPARROW

SIZE: 7 in (18 cm)

HABITAT: Edges of coniferous woods, in bogs and wet grassy areas, weed fields, brushy hillsides and swampy areas, also parks.

RANGE: Across Canada and eastern North America.

FOOD: Weed seeds, insects. At feeder loves oil seed and sunflower.

THE SONG

OH SWEET SWEET POVERTY POVERTY

NOTE SEQUENCE: A series of clear loud ringing whistles.

TIME OF SONG: Morning and evening.

OTHER BIRDS WITH SIMILAR SONG: Similar to the White-crowned Sparrow (Zonotrichia leucophrys), which has a shorter, less distinctly phrased song.

FOX SPARROW

SIZE: 7 inches (18cm)

HABITAT: Conifer and mixed woods, thickets, and shrubs.

RANGE: West coast down to Texas and North Carolina.

FOOD: Insects, seeds and fruits.

SONG SPARROW

SIZE: 5½–7 inches (14–18 cm)

HABITAT: Thickets, brushy areas, old fields, gardens.

RANGE: South from Nebraska to New Mexico, Texas, and Florida.

FOOD: Seeds and small insects.

WHITE-CROWNED SPARROW

SIZE: 6 inches (15 cm)

HABITAT: Bushy places, roadsides, woodland edges.

RANGE: South to Gulf states, Mexico, Cuba.

FOOD: Seeds, insects.

HOUSE SPARROW

SIZE: 5–6 inches (13–15 cm)

HABITAT: Gardens, parks, suburbs, farms.

RANGE: Almost all of North America.

FOOD: Insects, seeds, scraps.

BROWN-HEADED COWBIRD

SIZE: 7 inches (18 cm)

HABITAT: Farms, fields, roadsides, woodland edges.

RANGE: Southern Canada to Mexico, northern Florida.

FOOD: Insects, fruits, grain, seeds.

DARK-EYED JUNCO

SIZE: 5¼–6 inches (14–17 cm)

HABITAT: Conifers and mixed woods,
gardens, thickets, open ground in winter.

RANGE: South to Gulf states, Mexico.

FOOD: Insects, seeds, berries.

EASTERN KINGBIRD

SIZE: 8 in (20 cm)

HABITAT: Open areas such as field edges, forest clearings, farmlands, orchards, gardens; often near water.

RANGE: Northern New England west to northern British Columbia then south across the plains to eastern Texas and Florida.

FOOD: Winged insects, especially bees, occasionally berries.

THE SONG

KAZEEH KAHZEEH-KIP-KIP DZYPPER

NOTE SEQUENCE: A loud series of twitters and harsh notes.

TIME OF SONG: All day.

OTHER BIRDS WITH SIMILAR SONG: All Flycatchers have twittering notes, but none have a true sweet song.

EASTERN WOOD PEEWEE

SIZE: 6 ¼ in (16 cm)

HABITAT: Woodlands, orchards.

RANGE: Eastern half of the U.S. to northern Florida.

FOOD: Insects, which are snapped up as it sallies forth from a dead limb perch.

THE SONG

PEEE-A-WEEEEE PEE-A-WEEEEE

NOTE SEQUENCE: A loud, long drawn out and often mournful sound with a rising inflection at the end.

TIME OF SONG: All day throughout summer.

OTHER BIRDS WITH SIMILAR SONG: Some similarity to the breeding call of the Black-capped Chickadee (Poecile atricapillus).

DIPPER

SIZE: 7 ½ in (19 cm)

HABITAT: Rocky river and mountain streams.

RANGE: Western United States.

FOOD: Insects, invertebrates, small fish.

THE SONG

SEE-TA SI SI SI LA TE LASEE SEE

NOTE SEQUENCE: A fluid, bubbling flow of two main phrases, the first on a higher pitch.

TIME OF SONG: Morning and evening.

OTHER BIRDS WITH SIMILAR SONG: Similar to the prolonged song of Winter Wren (Troglodytes troglodytes), but much louder and more forceful.

BLUE-GRAY GNATCATCHER

SIZE: 4 ½ in (11 cm)

HABITAT: Mixed woodland, oak woods, chaparral, pinyon pine groves, dense hillside thickets.

RANGE: Northeastern U.S. west to California and south to Mexico.

FOOD: Mainly insects and other invertebrates.

THE SONG

SPIT-SEE SPIT-SEE SEE SEE TIDDLEEE SEE SEE

NOTE SEQUENCE: The call is high-pitched; the song a jubilant outpouring of lisps and warbled notes.

TIME OF SONG: All day.

OTHER BIRDS WITH SIMILAR SONG: Quite unlike any other bird's call.

EASTERN BLUEBIRD

SIZE: 7 in (18 cm)

HABITAT: Open woodland edges, farmland, orchards, gardens.

RANGE: Eastern half of the U.S.

FOOD: Mainly insects with some berries and seeds.

THE SONG

TA TA TEE O TA TA TOO LEE

NOTE SEQUENCE: A mellow series of notes usually sung at low level, sounds like a guttural warbling.

TIME OF SONG: Morning and evening.

OTHER BIRDS WITH SIMILAR SONG: The Western Bluebird and Mountain Bluebird (Sialia currucoides), also have gentle, warbled songs.

MOUNTAIN BLUEBIRD

SIZE: 7 ¼ in (18 cm)

HABITAT: Alpine meadows and mountain woodland.

RANGE: Western North America from south British Columbia to Arizona and on to Mexico.

FOOD: Small insects and invertebrates.

THE SONG

TUR-LEE TUR-LEE

NOTE SEQUENCE: A mellow series of notes usually sung at low level, sounds like a guttural warbling.

TIME OF SONG: Morning.

OTHER BIRDS WITH SIMILAR SONG: Similar to Western Bluebird and Eastern Bluebird (Sialia sialis).

VEERY

SIZE: 7 in (18 cm)

HABITAT: Wet uplands and mixed woods.

RANGE: Across north U.S. and south Canada.

FOOD: Flying insects such as dragonflies as well as beetles, grubs, slugs, and other invertebrates.

THE SONG

SEE TO SEE TOLEE TO WEE

NOTE SEQUENCE: A rolling series of descending notes that tumble downward with a flute-like quality.

TIME OF SONG: Morning and evening.

OTHER BIRDS WITH SIMILAR SONG: In quality like a Wood Thrush (Hylocichla mustelina), but it spirals downward.

SWAINSON'S THRUSH

SIZE: 7 in (18 cm)

HABITAT: Cool northern forests or mixed woods on migration.

RANGE: Alaska across Canada, south into the Rockies and northeast U.S.

FOOD: Wide variety of small insects, larvae, seeds, and berries.

THE SONG

TEE-TWAOO-TEE EE TA LEE

NOTE SEQUENCE: A series of ascending whistles.

TIME OF SONG: Morning and evening.

OTHER BIRDS WITH SIMILAR SONG: The Gray-checked Thrush song is very similar but spirals down at the end.

HERMIT THRUSH

SIZE: 6-6 ¾ in (15-17 cm)

HABITAT: Evergreen forests, bogs, swamps.

RANGE: Across north North America from Alaska to Newfoundland and south in western and eastern mountains.

FOOD: Insects, worms, small snails, berries, and seeds. Has visited feeders on rare occasions.

THE SONG

OO LA LA LOW/AH LA LA/AY I A LA/LA LEE

NOTE SEQUENCE: Pairs of flutelike notes rising and falling, ending with two-toned trills.

TIME OF SONG: Morning and evening.

OTHER BIRDS WITH SIMILAR SONG: Wood Thrush (Hylocichla mustelina), has a similar flute-like song but lacks prolonged trills.

WOOD THRUSH

SIZE: 7 ¾ in (20 cm)

HABITAT: Prefers the cool understory near brooklets, swamp edges, and wet ravines.

RANGE: Throughout eastern North America.

FOOD: Insects, spiders, worms, some berries.

THE SONG

EE-OH-LAY-EE-OH-LEE

NOTE SEQUENCE: A beautiful two-toned flute-like song.

TIME OF SONG: Morning and evening.

OTHER BIRDS WITH SIMILAR SONG: Similar to a Hermit Thrush (Catharus guttatus), but phrases are shorter and more spiraling.

VARIED THRUSH

SIZE: 9 ½ in (24 cm)

HABITAT: Dense coniferous forests.

RANGE: Western North America from Alaska to California.

FOOD: Insects and earthworms.

THE SONG

WHEEEEE WHEEE WHEEE WHEEE

NOTE SEQUENCE: A series of drawn-out buzzing whistles, each delivered on a different pitch.

TIME OF SONG: Morning and evening.

OTHER BIRDS WITH SIMILAR SONG: A unique song unlike any other thrush.

TOWNSEND'S SOLITAIRE

SIZE: 8 ½ in (22 cm)

HABITAT: Cool northern evergreen forests, rocky hillsides, and ravines.

RANGE: West coast from Alaska to Mexico through the Rockies.

FOOD: Wide variety of insects, berries, and seeds.

THE SONG

TOO WEE TOO WERE-TOO WEE TO SEE TEE TWEER

NOTE SEQUENCE: Long in duration; sweet, clear notes often delivered in flight. Also a loud "yeek" note.

TIME OF SONG: Morning and evening.

OTHER BIRDS WITH SIMILAR SONG: Some explosive notes of Flycatcher sound like "eek" note of this bird.

MOCKINGBIRD

SIZE: 11 in (28 cm)

HABITAT: Gardens, farmlands, parks, back-yards. Any brushy areas. Multiflora rose is a key shrub.

RANGE: New England across the lower Great Plains to California and south to Mexico.

FOOD: Wild berries, especially rosehips, seeds, insects, and other invertebrates. Rare at feeder.

THE SONG

ﾉﾉ⌣⌣^~ﾉﾉ

RICK CHICK CHICK WEE

NOTE SEQUENCE: Harsh paired calls rising and falling in a see-saw manner. During the spring, often sings all night.

TIME OF SONG: All day.

OTHER BIRDS WITH SIMILAR SONG: Brown Thrasher (Toxostoma rufum), sounds similar but always sings in double phrases.

GRAY CATBIRD

SIZE: 8 ½ in (22 cm)

HABITAT: Forest understory, thickets, gardens, backyards.

RANGE: Eastern half of the U.S., lower Canada and spreading west to Colorado.

FOOD: About half animal matter — insects and their larvae — and half plant material — berries and seeds. At feeder takes orange halves and raisins.

THE SONG

COYAT EEE ELA TOOLEE TEE TA TEE

NOTE SEQUENCE: A jumbled series of notes, often harsh and with prolonged lispy endings. Distinct "mew."

TIME OF SONG: All day.

OTHER BIRDS WITH SIMILAR SONG: Similar to a Brown Thrasher (Toxostoma rufum), but song not given in couplets.

BROWN THRASHER

SIZE: 11 ½ in (29 cm)

HABITAT: Brushy edges, thickets, ravines, woodland tangles.

RANGE: Eastern two-thirds of the U.S. and south Canada.

FOOD: Insects, other small invertebrates, some fruits and seeds.

THE SONG

TWEE-TWEE TOYOU-TOYOU CHACK-CHACK

WHEEP-WHEEP

NOTE SEQUENCE: Always delivered in couplets which alternate between harsh notes and sweet whistles.

TIME OF SONG: Morning and evening.

OTHER BIRDS WITH SIMILAR SONG: Similar to Catbird (Dumetella carolinensis), and Mockingbird (Mimus polyglottos), but delivered in couplets.

WATER PIPIT

SIZE: 7 in (18 cm)

HABITAT: Open country, tundra, mountains above the tree line, fields, coastal flats.

RANGE: Breeds in high Arctic and mountains of Alaska and the Rockies.

FOOD: Insects and small invertebrates such as beach fleas.

THE SONG

PIP-PIP-PIPIT CHEEDLE ZEE

NOTE SEQUENCE: High-pitched whistled notes followed by a thin, lisping series. When flushed delivers pip-pip-it call.

TIME OF SONG: All day.

OTHER BIRDS WITH SIMILAR SONG: Hard to confuse it with any other bird except Sprague's Pipit, which has a musical, twittering quality.

WARBLING VIREO

SIZE: 5 ½ in (14 cm)

HABITAT: Large trees of upland woods, riverine forest, parks; tends to stay in upper branches.

RANGE: Throughout most of the U.S. and western Canada.

FOOD: Insects.

THE SONG

TWEE-TWEE TOOSEE TOOMEE TOOSEE

NOTE SEQUENCE: Long series of melodic warbles dropping at the end.

TIME OF SONG: All day.

OTHER BIRDS WITH SIMILAR SONG: The Yellow-throated Vireo's song is similar but more raspy.

RED-EYED VIREO

SIZE: 6 in (15 cm)

HABITAT: Secondary growth woodlands with shrubby understory, also orchards, parks.

RANGE: Across Canada, eastern U.S. and northern portion of western U.S.

FOOD: Mainly insects and small invertebrates.

THE SONG

TOO LEE TEE A TOO TOO LA TOO

NOTE SEQUENCE: A series of two-parted whistles that rock back and forth.

TIME OF SONG: All day.

OTHER BIRDS WITH SIMILAR SONG: Very similar to Blue-headed Vireo, which has a slower-paced song.

BELL'S VIREO

SIZE: 4 ¾ in (12 cm)

HABITAT: Wet woods, especially riverine willow shrubberies and mesquite thickets.

RANGE: Central plains south through Texas and west through Arizona.

FOOD: Insects.

THE SONG

CHEEDLE CHEEDLE CHEEDLE CHEEDLE

NOTE SEQUENCE: Sounds like a question and answer sequence.

TIME OF SONG: Morning and evening.

OTHER BIRDS WITH SIMILAR SONG: Hutton's Vireo has a similar song sequence but is less rhythmic.

AMERICAN CROW

SIZE: 21½ inches (55 cm)

HABITAT: Woods, parks, farmlands.

RANGE: North America, from south Canada to New Mexico.

FOOD: Omnivorous.

BLACK-CAPPED CHICKADEE

SIZE: 4½ inches (11.5 cm)

HABITAT: Mixed and deciduous woods, thickets, gardens.

RANGE: Alaska, central and southern Canada, northern half of U.S.

FOOD: Insects, seeds.

OAK TITMOUSE

SIZE: 5¼ inches (14 cm)

HABITAT: Conifers and deciduous woodlands, and scrub.

RANGE: California and Mexico; just reaching Oregon.

FOOD: Small insects, seeds, nuts, berries.

BOREAL CHICKADEE

SIZE: 5 ½ in (14 cm)

HABITAT: Northern coniferous forests.

RANGE: Canada and Alaska.

FOOD: Insects, their eggs and larvae, and spiders.

THE SONG

SEEK-A-DAY-DAY SEE-YOU

NOTE SEQUENCE: Call is repetitious with accented rise at the end; song is a repeated warble.

TIME OF SONG: All day.

OTHER BIRDS WITH SIMILAR SONG: The call of the Black-capped Chickadee (Poecile atricapillus), is less accented and emphatic.

TUFTED TITMOUSE

SIZE: 6 in (15 cm)

HABITAT: Woodlands, swamplands, orchards, parks, backyards.

RANGE: Eastern half of U.S., range expanding.

FOOD: Seventy percent of diet is insects, also seeds and berries. At feeder, favorites are peanut butter and seeds.

THE SONG

PETER-PETER-PETER

NOTE SEQUENCE: A loud and ringing staccato series, with loud whistles.

TIME OF SONG: All day.

OTHER BIRDS WITH SIMILAR SONG: Parts of song can be mistaken for chickadee notes.

EASTERN PHOEBE

SIZE: 7 in (18 cm)

HABITAT: Woodlands, parks, gardens, backyards; common around buildings.

RANGE: Eastern portion of North America from the Great Plains to north New England and south to eastern Texas and northern Florida.

FOOD: Mainly insects and spiders with berries in winter.

THE SONG

FEE-BEEP FEE-BEEP FEE-BEEP

NOTE SEQUENCE: Emphatic and two-parted with a sharp inflection upward on the second part.

TIME OF SONG: Morning.

OTHER BIRDS WITH SIMILAR SONG: In spring, the Black-capped Chickadee gives a loud "feee-bee" whistle, but not the sharp "phoe-bee" of this Flycatcher.

SAY'S PHOEBE

SIZE: 7-8 in (18-20 cm)

HABITAT: Open and rocky country.

RANGE: A wide range from central Alaska to the edge of the plains and south to the Arizona/west Texas border.

FOOD: Insects, and will glean spiders from rock surfaces, berries taken in winter.

THE SONG

_ / _ / _ /

PEE-YEET PEE-YEET

NOTE SEQUENCE: Explosive and upward pitched.

TIME OF SONG: Mainly morning and near dusk.

OTHER BIRDS WITH SIMILAR SONG: Similar in sequence to Vermillion Flycatcher (Pyrocephalus rubinus), but much louder.

OVENBIRD

SIZE: 6 in (15 cm)

HABITAT: Mixed woodland.

RANGE: Most of southern Canada, south through the midwest to the Carolina coast.

FOOD: Insects and other invertebrates.

THE SONG

TEACHER-TEACHER-TEACHER-TEACHER

NOTE SEQUENCE: A loud series of distinct phrases rising in intensity. Also a more gushing evening song.

TIME OF SONG: Morning and evening.

OTHER BIRDS WITH SIMILAR SONG: Pulsing song is not to be confused with any others.

LOUISIANA WATERTHRUSH

SIZE: 6 in (15 cm)

HABITAT: Breeds near flowing streams; other wet areas on migration.

RANGE: Eastern half of the U.S. from New England to north Florida.

FOOD: Invertebrates such as worms, as well as insects and their larvae.

THE SONG

SEE-SEE-SEE-TOO LA SEE DE

NOTE SEQUENCE: Two-parted, introduced by three clear whistled notes followed by a rapid series of clear bubbling notes rolling down the scale.

TIME OF SONG: Morning and evening.

OTHER BIRDS WITH SIMILAR SONG: Similar to a Northern Waterthrush but not as rapid and with more introductory notes.

COMMON YELLOWTHROAT

SIZE: 5 in (13 cm)

HABITAT: Damp fields, dense thickets, cattail marshes, mangroves in South.

RANGE: United States and southern Canada.

FOOD: Insects.

THE SONG

TWITCHITY TWITCHITY TWITCHITY

NOTE SEQUENCE: Series of rapid explosive calls with an emphasis on the first part: twitch---ity.

TIME OF SONG: All day.

OTHER BIRDS WITH SIMILAR SONG: The Yellow Warbler (Dendroica petechia), has a rollicking song but not as emphatic.

YELLOW-BREASTED CHAT

SIZE: 7 ½ in (19 cm)

HABITAT: Thickets, wood edges, powerlines.

RANGE: Most of the U.S. except portions of the plains.

FOOD: Insects, spiders.

THE SONG

CHACK-CHACK REE CHIP CHIP TWEE TWEE

NOTE SEQUENCE: A jumbled series of hacking and whistled notes of no set pattern, often delivered at night.

TIME OF SONG: Day and night.

OTHER BIRDS WITH SIMILAR SONG: Could be confused with a Brown Thrasher (Toxostoma rufum), but Thrashers always in duplicate couplets.

SUMMER TANAGER

SIZE: 7 ½ in (19 cm)

HABITAT: Pine woodlands and mixed oak woodlands, swampy areas.

RANGE: Southeastern and southwestern U.S.

FOOD: Insects including bees and wasps.

THE SONG

PEE-TUCK-I-TUCK/SEAR-TO-WHEER

TO SEAR TOO WHEAR

NOTE SEQUENCE: Call is sharp, the song is harsh and raspy. Languid, see-saw phrases.

TIME OF SONG: Morning and evening.

OTHER BIRDS WITH SIMILAR SONG: Similar to Scarlet Tanager (Piranga olivacea), which is more raspy and choppy.

SCARLET TANAGER

SIZE: 7 in (18 cm)

HABITAT: Upland woods of oak, hickory, and maple, riverine forest.

RANGE: Northeastern North America.

FOOD: Mainly insects, especially caterpillars, also some berries and seeds.

THE SONG

HURRY, TO WORRY, FLURRY, ITS BLURRY

CHIP-BURR

NOTE SEQUENCE: A series of harsh, coarse notes in rapid succession.

TIME OF SONG: All day.

OTHER BIRDS WITH SIMILAR SONG: Like a Summer Tanager but harsher and more see-saw in tone.

WESTERN TANAGER

SIZE: 7¼ inches (18 cm)

HABITAT: Coniferous forests.

RANGE: Western North America.

FOOD: Insects and berries.

LAZULI BUNTING

SIZE: 5½ inches (14 cm)

HABITAT: Brushy areas, thickets, backyards.

RANGE: Northern Arizona and New Mexico.

FOOD: Seeds, insects.

EVENING GROSBEAK

SIZE: 7–8 inches (18–20 cm)

HABITAT: Conifers, shrubs, gardens.

RANGE: Southward to Mexico.

FOOD: Seeds, fruits, berries.

ROSE-BREASTED GROSBEAK

SIZE: 8 in (20 cm)

HABITAT: Open deciduous woodlands, parks, orchards, thickets.

RANGE: Western and south Canada south to midwest and mid-Atlantic states.

FOOD: Mixed insects and vegetable diet. Attracted to fruit blossom in spring, fruit and seeds in fall and winter.

THE SONG

TOODLE LOO TWEEDLE LEET TA DO

NOTE SEQUENCE: Rapid sequence of clear whistled notes; in the fall a squeaking eek call.

TIME OF SONG: Morning and evening.

OTHER BIRDS WITH SIMILAR SONG: Very similar to the Black-headed Grosbeak (Pheucticus melanocephalus), but on a higher pitch.

BLACK-HEADED GROSBEAK

SIZE: 7 ½ in (19 cm)

HABITAT: Mixed woodlands, streamside edges, orchards, gardens.

RANGE: Western U.S. from British Columbia south to Mexico and east to the Dakotas, Nebraska, and west to Texas.

FOOD: Various fruits and seeds; at feeder prefers sunflower seeds.

THE SONG

TO-WE — TO WEER TO WEET-TEE TO WHEER

NOTE SEQUENCE: A long series of clear whistles.

TIME OF SONG: Morning.

OTHER BIRDS WITH SIMILAR SONG: Very similar to Rose-breasted Grosbeak (Pheucticus ludovicianus), but lower in pitch.

BLUE GROSBEAK

SIZE: 6-7 ½ in (15-19 cm)

HABITAT: Fields, hedgerows, thickets, woodland edges, roadside brush.

RANGE: Southern U.S. to Costa Rica; winters in southern part of range.

FOOD: Insects, seeds, and fruit at ground level and in trees.

PINE GROSBEAK

SIZE: 8 in (20 cm)

HABITAT: Coniferous and scrub forest.

RANGE: Northern and Western North America.

FOOD: Berries and buds.

DICKCISSEL

SIZE: 6-7 in (15-18 cm)

HABITAT: Grasslands and weedy fields.

RANGE: The Midwest.

FOOD: Grass seeds, grains, insects. At feeder oil seed, sunflower, and fine cracked corn.

THE SONG

DICK DICK CIC CIC CIC SEL SEL

NOTE SEQUENCE: A rhythmic unmusical series of wispy buzzy notes.

TIME OF SONG: All day.

OTHER BIRDS WITH SIMILAR SONG: Similar to the Savannah Sparrow which lacks the distinct pulsing introduction.

GREEN-TAILED TOWHEE

SIZE: 7 in (18 cm)

HABITAT: Dense shrubs of high plateau country.

RANGE: High plateau country of the West.

FOOD: Wide variety of seeds, fruit, and some insects.

THE SONG

SWEET-OOOOO

NOTE SEQUENCE: Opens with a clear, whistled sweet-oooo followed by a series of jumbled notes with a raspy central portion.

TIME OF SONG: All day.

OTHER BIRDS WITH SIMILAR SONG: Gray Catbird (Dumetella carolinensis), Fox Sparrow (Passerella iliaca).

EASTERN TOWHEE

SIZE: 8 in (20 cm)

HABITAT: Dry woods and riverside thickets, weedy hillsides, chaparral, parks.

RANGE: Eastern half of the U.S.

FOOD: Seeds and insects.

THE SONG

CHEWINK/DRINK YOUR TEA

NOTE SEQUENCE: A distinct call, and a loud clear song with the ending drawn out.

TIME OF SONG: All day.

OTHER BIRDS WITH SIMILAR SONG: The Spotted Towhee — its western counterpart — is near identical.

HORNED LARK

SIZE: 7 in (18 cm)

HABITAT: Tundra, alpine areas, shorelines, agricultural land.

RANGE: Widespread throughout North America from Alaska to the Mexican Border.

FOOD: Seeds, insects, and other small invertebrates.

THE SONG

PEET TWEEDLE EE DEE DEET

NOTE SEQUENCE: A soft tinkling series of notes usually delivered from high overhead.

TIME OF SONG: All day.

OTHER BIRDS WITH SIMILAR SONG: The tinkling notes of Tree Swallows (Tachycineta bicolor), might be confused with this species.

BROWN CREEPER

SIZE: 5 in (13 cm)

HABITAT: Mixed woods and pines.

RANGE: Across the U.S. and south Canada.

FOOD: Gleans bark for small insects, their egg cases, and larvae, also spiders and a few seeds; at feeder will take suet.

THE SONG

SEET-TWEEDLEE-DEET

NOTE SEQUENCE: A high-pitched short series, delivered very rapidly.

TIME OF SONG: Morning and evening.

OTHER BIRDS WITH SIMILAR SONG: Similar to the trilled song of Golden-crowned Kinglet but more musical.

COMMON GRACKLE

SIZE: 10–12 inches (25–30 cm)

HABITAT: Farms, towns, woodland edge.

RANGE: Southern two-thirds of U.S. east of Rockies.

FOOD: Insects, invertebrates, fruit, berries.

YELLOW-HEADED BLACKBIRD

SIZE: 9½ inches (24 cm)

HABITAT: Freshwater reed and cattail marshes.

RANGE: Western Canada and the U.S.

FOOD: Insects, seeds.

RED-WINGED BLACKBIRD

SIZE: Male 8–9½ inches (20–24 cm);
Female 7–7½ inches (18–19 cm)

HABITAT: Marshes, watercourses, cultivated land, wood edge.

RANGE: North and Central America.

FOOD: Insects, invertebrates, seeds.

RUSTY BLACKBIRD

SIZE: 9 in (23 cm)

HABITAT: Almost always near water, boggy edges of northern coniferous woods.

RANGE: Alaska through northern Canada, winters southeastern U.S.

FOOD: Insects and their larvae, spiders, seeds, and berries. Will visit feeder for seeds with other blackbird flocks.

THE SONG

CHACK CHACK CHACK/KISH-LAY

NOTE SEQUENCE: A short repeated rattle-like call; song is harsh and squeaky.

TIME OF SONG: All day.

OTHER BIRDS WITH SIMILAR SONG: Like short, harsh Red-winged Blackbird (Agelaius phoeniceus).

PINE SISKIN

SIZE: 4–5 inches (10–13 cm)

HABITAT: Conifers, mixed woods, bushy places.

RANGE: Southward to Mexico.

FOOD: Seeds, insects.

AMERICAN GOLDFINCH

SIZE: 4–5 inches (10–13 cm)

HABITAT: Weedy places, gardens, parks, roadsides, woodland edges.

RANGE: Canadian border through U.S. into northern Mexico.

FOOD: Seeds.

PURPLE FINCH

SIZE: 5–6 inches (13–15 cm)

HABITAT: Woods, groves, suburbs in winter.

RANGE: Widespread across U.S.

FOOD: Seeds.

HOUSE FINCH

SIZE: 5–6 inches (13–15 cm)

HABITAT: Cities, suburbs, gardens, farms.

RANGE: Widespread in western U.S., spreading locally in east.

FOOD: Seeds.

PYRRHULOXIA

SIZE: 8 ¾ in (22 cm)

HABITAT: Weedy thickets, grassland edges, gardens.

RANGE: Extreme southwest U.S. and western and southern Texas.

FOOD: Wide variety of seeds; will visit feeder for oil, sunflower seed, and cracked corn.

THE SONG

SEE-TOO SEE-TOO — PEW YOU PEW YOU

NOTE SEQUENCE: A series of thin whistles and rapid chirps.

TIME OF SONG: Morning and evening.

OTHER BIRDS WITH SIMILAR SONG: Northern Cardinal (Cardinalis cardinalis), but thinner and not as rapid.

NORTHERN CARDINAL

SIZE: 9 in (23 cm)

HABITAT: Backyards, thickets, farmland, overgrown fields, woodland edge, parks.

RANGE: Eastern North America and from west Texas along the border through Arizona.

FOOD: The large bill is designed to crack open seeds and nuts; fruits, insects, and invertebrates also taken. Visits feeder readily for sunflower seeds.

THE SONG

WHEET WHEET WHEET PURTTY PURTTY PURTTY

CHEW CHEW CHEW

NOTE SEQUENCE: A loud clear ringing series of whistles.

TIME OF SONG: Morning and evening.

OTHER BIRDS WITH SIMILAR SONG: Individual whistled notes of Tufted Titmouse (Baeolophus bicolor), can cause confusion.

RED CROSSBILL

SIZE: 6 ½ in (17 cm)

HABITAT: Coniferous woodlands.

RANGE: Across Canada and southwestern U.S. mountains to Mexico.

FOOD: Seeds of conifers, also other fruits and seeds (maple, beech, ash). Will visit feeder for sunflower and thistle seeds; insects eaten in late spring.

THE SONG

— — — — —

JIP-JIP-JIP JIP-JIP-JIP

NOTE SEQUENCE: The distinctive call consists of a series of sharp notes, while the song is a softer too-tee too-tee too-tee tee tee.

TIME OF SONG: Morning.

OTHER BIRDS WITH SIMILAR SONG: Close to White-winged Crossbill, which has a harsh chit chit call.

BOBOLINK

SIZE: 7 in (18 cm)

HABITAT: Fields, meadows.

RANGE: Northern U.S. and southern Canada.

FOOD: Seeds, insects.

THE SONG

BOB-O-LINK-LINK-LINCOLN

NOTE SEQUENCE: A bubbly outpouring of metallic and warbled notes with a rolling pattern increasing in speed as it nears the end.

TIME OF SONG: All day.

OTHER BIRDS WITH SIMILAR SONG: Unique and shouldn't be confused with any others.

EASTERN MEADOWLARK

SIZE: 10 in (25 cm)

HABITAT: Grasslands, prairies, farmland.

RANGE: Eastern two-thirds of U.S.

FOOD: Wide range of insects, grass and weed seeds; in marshy areas also takes young snails.

THE SONG

TEE-TWEEDLE EE DO

NOTE SEQUENCE: A loud series of high-pitched whistles and warbles.

TIME OF SONG: All day.

OTHER BIRDS WITH SIMILAR SONG: Like Western Meadowlark but shorter in duration and less bubbly.

BALTIMORE ORIOLE

SIZE: 8 ½ in (22 cm)

HABITAT: Open woodlands, riverine forest, shade trees in parks, yards, orchards, and gardens.

RANGE: Eastern half of North America.

FOOD: Principally insects including hairy caterpillars, with some fruit and seeds; fruits taken in winter, when it will also take suet at feeder.

THE SONG

WEE WEE-TOO LEE TOO/CHECK-CHECK CHECK

NOTE SEQUENCE: Introduced by clear whistles followed by a triplet of short whistled phrases; call is harsh and rapid.

TIME OF SONG: Morning and evening.

OTHER BIRDS WITH SIMILAR SONG: Like the similar Bullock's Oriole but more liquid.

ORCHARD ORIOLE

SIZE: 7 in (18 cm)

HABITAT: Shade trees, orchards, riverine forest, open woodland, parks.

RANGE: Eastern half of U.S.

FOOD: Mainly insects, spiders, some berries, and seeds. Attracted to feeder by water.

THE SONG

WHAT-CHEER-KALEE KALEE-TOLEE

TOLEE-TOLAY WHAT-CHEER

NOTE SEQUENCE: A rolling bubbly series introduced or ending with a distinctive what-cheer.

TIME OF SONG: Morning and evening.

OTHER BIRDS WITH SIMILAR SONG: Similar to Baltimore Oriole (Icterus galbula), but more bubbly and sweet whistles.

LARK BUNTING

SIZE: 7 in (18 cm)

HABITAT: Sagebrush, prairie, grasslands, agricultural land.

RANGE: Great Plains of the U.S. and south central Canada.

FOOD: Wide variety of seeds.

THE SONG

WHO-LEE SWEET SWEET SWEET

NOTE SEQUENCE: A jumble of whistles, trills, and harsher notes.

TIME OF SONG: Morning and evening.

OTHER BIRDS WITH SIMILAR SONG: Somewhat like the McCowen's Longspur, which nests in the same habitat.

AMERICAN WHITE PELICAN

SIZE: 50–70 in (127–178 cm)

HABITAT: Freshwater lakes and shallow coastal waters.

RANGE: North America.

FOOD: Fish.

BROWN PELICAN

SIZE: 43–54 in (110–137 cm)

HABITAT: Shallow coastal waters and islands.

RANGE: Pacific and Atlantic coasts of North and South America; Galapagos Islands.

FOOD: Fish.

AMERICAN DARTER

SIZE: 34 in (86 cm)

HABITAT: Inland and brackish waters; can occur on coasts.

RANGE: Southeastern U.S. to Northern South America.

FOOD: Fish and aquatic vertebrates.

AMERICAN BITTERN

SIZE: 25 in (64 cm)

HABITAT: Fresh and saltwater marshes, swamps and bogs.

RANGE: Central Canada to Central U.S.; winters Southern U.S., Caribbean, Mexico, Central America.

FOOD: Insects and fish.

SNOW GOOSE

SIZE: 25 ½ –33 in (65–84 cm)

HABITAT: Breeds on Arctic tundra; winters on freshwater and salt marshes, farmland

RANGE: Arctic North America; winters on both seaboards and south to Gulf of Mexico.

FOOD: Seeds, leaves, and grasses.

HAWAIIAN GOOSE

SIZE: 22–28 in (56–71 cm)

HABITAT: Sparsely vegetated slopes of volcanoes.

RANGE: Confined to the Hawaiian Islands.

FOOD: Leaves, grasses, and berries.

SHARP-SHINNED HAWK

SIZE: 10–14 inches (25–36 cm); female larger

HABITAT: Woods, parks, gardens, farmland with trees.

RANGE: Northern U.S. southward.

FOOD: Small birds.

RED-SHOULDERED HAWK

SIZE: 16–20 in (41–51 cm)

HABITAT: Mixed or deciduous woodland and nearby open country.

RANGE: North America, southern to central Mexico.

FOOD: Small mammals, birds, and snakes.

RED-TAILED HAWK

SIZE: 16–18 in (41–46 cm)

HABITAT: Extremely varied, but usually with some tree cover.

RANGE: North and Central America, Caribbean.

FOOD: Small mammals, birds, and reptiles.

OSPREY

SIZE: 21 ½ in-23 in (55-58 cm)

HABITAT: Coasts, rivers, lakes, wetlands.

RANGE: Breeds North America, Eurasia (mainly migrants), NE Africa, Australia; winter visitor and non-breeding migrant elsewhere.

FOOD: Fish.

AMERICAN SWALLOW-TAILED KITE

SIZE: 23 ½ in (60 cm)

HABITAT: Woodland and forest.

RANGE: Southeastern U.S., Mexico south to northern Argentina.

FOOD: Small reptiles and birds.

juvenile

BALD EAGLE

SIZE: 31–37 in (79–94 cm)

HABITAT: Usually near lakes, rivers, coasts.

RANGE: North America.

FOOD: Birds, small mammals, and fish.

COMMON TURKEY

SIZE: male 48 in (122 cm); female 34 in (86 cm)

HABITAT: Forests, clearings, brushland.

RANGE: U.S., Mexico.

FOOD: Seeds, nuts, berries, small animals.

NORTHERN BOBWHITE

SIZE: 8–11 in (20–28 cm)

HABITAT: Open pine forests, clearings.

RANGE: Eastern U.S. to southwestern U.S. and Mexico.

FOOD: Seeds and fruits of grasses, shrubs, and crops.

MONTEZUMA QUAIL

SIZE: 7 in (18 cm)

HABITAT: Open, grassy, pine, juniper, and oak woodland.

RANGE: Southern Arizona, New Mexico, Texas, northern Mexico.

FOOD: Seeds and insects.

SANDHILL CRANE

SIZE: 42 in (107 cm)

HABITAT: Tundra, marshes, grassland, fields.

RANGE: Breeds northeastern Siberia, Alaska, Canada, northern U.S.; winters southern U.S. to central Mexico; small resident populations in Florida and Mississippi, Cuba.

FOOD: Plants, insects, worms, frogs, and small mammals.

AMERICAN BLACK OYSTERCATCHER

SIZE: 15 in (38 cm)

HABITAT: Rocky coasts and islands, occasionally sandy beaches.

RANGE: Pacific coast of North America, from Alaska to Baja California.

FOOD: Mollusks and marine creatures.

SPOTTED SANDPIPER

SIZE: 7 ½ in (19 cm)

HABITAT: Open and wooded areas, usually near water.

RANGE: Breeds North America; winters south from Mexico to southern Brazil.

FOOD: Insects and small crustaceans.

AMERICAN KESTREL

SIZE: 8½ inches (22 cm)

HABITAT: Parks, gardens, open fields, bushy areas, woodland edge.

RANGE: Most of North and South America.

FOOD: Small rodents, insects, small birds.

RING-BILLED GULL

SIZE: 16 inches (41 cm)

HABITAT: Lakes, quays and beaches, farmland.

RANGE: Coasts, southern U.S. to Gulf, Mexico, Cuba.

FOOD: Fish, scraps, worms.

GREAT BLACK-BACKED GULL

SIZE: 28–31 in (71–79 cm)

HABITAT: Coasts, locally inland waters and moors.

RANGE: Coastal northeastern North America.

FOOD: Seabirds and rabbits.

FRANKLIN'S GULL

SIZE: 13–15 in (33–38 cm)

HABITAT: Breeds in freshwater marshes; winters on coasts.

RANGE: Breeds on North American prairies; winters on coasts of Central and South America.

FOOD: Invertebrates.

AMERICAN BLACK DUCK

SIZE: 21–24 in (53–61 cm)

HABITAT: Freshwater marshes in woods; winters on estuaries, coastal marshes.

RANGE: Northeastern North America; winters south to Gulf of Mexico.

FOOD: Seeds and mussels.

NORTHERN PINTAIL

SIZE: male 25–29 in (63–74 cm) including 4-in (10-cm) central tail feathers; female 17–25 in (43–63 cm)

HABITAT: Open marshes; winters on estuaries and coastal lagoons.

RANGE: Eurasia and North America; winters south to Panama, central Africa, India, Philippines.

FOOD: Plant roots and leaves.

MALLARD

SIZE: 16 inches (41 cm)

HABITAT: Water, especially freshwater, waterside areas.

RANGE: Almost all of North America.

FOOD: Seeds, shoots, aquatic vegetation, invertebrates.

AMERICAN COOT

SIZE: 12 inches (30 cm)

HABITAT: Lakes, reservoirs, rivers, parks, ponds.

RANGE: Canada to Ecuador.

FOOD: Aquatic plants and invertebrates.

GREATER ROADRUNNER

SIZE: 20–24 in (51–61 cm)

HABITAT: Semi-desert, chaparral, grassland, farmland, occasionally moist woodland.

RANGE: Western U.S., east to Louisiana, south to southern Mexico.

FOOD: Small animals.

GREAT HORNED OWL

SIZE: 20 inches (51 cm)

HABITAT: Forests, woodlands, thickets, open country with scattered trees.

RANGE: Alaska south throughout Americas.

FOOD: Rodents and larger mammals, birds.

BARN OWL

SIZE: 13–14 in (33–35 cm)

HABITAT: Mainly open or semi-open lowlands, including farmland.

RANGE: Americas, Europe, Africa, Arabia, India, Southeast Asia, Australia.

FOOD: Rodents.

NORTHERN PYGMY OWL

SIZE: 6 ½ in (17 cm)

HABITAT: Dense woodland in mountains and foothills.

RANGE: Western North America (north to Alaska, east to Rocky Mountains) south to Guatemala.

FOOD: Rodents, birds, and insects.

BIRD FINDER AT A GLANCE

American Kestrel

Ring-billed Gull

Rock Pigeon

Chimney Swift

Ruby-throated Hummingbird

Red-bellied Woodpecker

Northern Flicker

Purple Martin

Blue Jay

California Scrub-Jay

Double-crested Cormorant

Mallard

American Coot

Sharp-shinned Hawk

Mourning Dove

Yellow-billed Cuckoo

271

Great Horned Owl

Red-headed Woodpecker

Hairy Woodpecker

Tree Swallow

Barn Swallow

American Crow

Horned Lark

Gray jay

Black-capped Chickadee

Boreal Chickadee

Oak Titmouse

White-breasted Nuthatch

Tufted Titmouse

Red-breasted Nuthatch

Brown Creeper

Canyon Wren

Cactus Wren

Eastern Kingbird

Eastern Wood Pewee

Eastern Phoebe

Say's Phoebe

Great-Crested Flycatcher

Olive-Sided Flycatcher

Vermillion Flycatcher

Willow Flycatcher

House Wren

Winter Wren

Bewick's Wren

Marsh Wren

Dipper

Blue-Gray Gnatcatcher

Eastern Bluebird

Golden-Crowned Kinglet

Ruby-Crowned Kinglet

American Robin

Mountain Bluebird

Veery

Swainson's Thrush

Hermit Thrush

Wood Thrush

Varied Thrush

Townsend's Solitaire

Mockingbird

Gray Catbird

Brown Thrasher

Loggerhead Shrike

Cedar Waxwing

White-Crowned Sparrow

House Sparrow

Brown-Headed Cowbird

Kentucky Warbler

Northern Parula Warbler

Yellow Warbler

Chestnut-Sided Warbler

Black-Throated Warbler

Pine Warbler

Blackpoll Warbler

Black-and-White Warbler

Wilson's Warbler

Prothonotary Warbler

Connecticut Warbler

Louisiana Waterthrush

Ovenbird

Common Yellowthroat

Yellow-Breasted Chat

Pine Siskin

American Goldfinch

Purple Finch

House Finch

Rusty Blackbird

Bobolink

Eastern Meadowlark

Baltimore Oriole

Orchard Oriole

American Redstart

Wrentit

Water Pipit

Warbling Vireo

Red-eyed Vireo

Bell's Vireo

Yellow-rumped Warbler

European Starling

Lark Bunting

Red Crossbill

Indigo Bunting

Dickcissel

Green-tailed Towhee

Eastern Towhee

Bachman's Sparrow

Tree Sparrow

Chipping Sparrow

Fox Sparrow

Henslow's Sparrow

Vesper Sparrow

White-throated Sparrow

Song Sparrow

Dark-eyed Junco

Common Grackle

Yellow-headed Blackbird

Red-winged Blackbird

Lazuli Bunting

Western Tanager

Scarlet Tanager

Summer Tanager

Pyrrhuloxia

Northern Cardinal

Rose-breasted Grosbeak

Black-headed Grosbeak

Evening Grosbeak

GLOSSARY

ABRASION Wear and tear on feathers, often removing paler spots and fringes and fading darker colors.

ALBINISM A lack of pigment: true albinos are white with pink eyes, but most "white" birds are partial albinos, or albinistic, with patches of white and normal eye colors.

AXILLARIES The feathers under the base of the wing, in the "wingpit." Also known as axillars.

BAND A metal band placed around a bird's leg, with an individual number; when the bird is caught or found dead, its movements can be traced. Also known as a ring.

BASTARD WING A tuft of feathers on the "thumb," halfway along the leading edge of the wing, which can be raised or lowered to control airflow in flight. Also called the alula.

BEAK Synonymous with bill; the two jaws and their horny covering.

BINOCULAR VISION The ability to see an area with both eyes; birds such as owls have forward-facing eyes, giving the greatest extent of binocular vision.

BIRD OF PREY Usually refers to daytime birds of prey, including eagles, vultures, hawks, falcons, harriers, and kites; may be used to include owls. Also called "raptors," or raptorial birds.

BLIND A small shelter from which to observe birds while remaining hidden from view. Also known as a hide.

BROOD A set of young birds hatched from one clutch of eggs.

CALL NOTE A vocalization, usually characteristic of the species, made to maintain contact, warn of danger, or for other specific purposes.

CAP A patch of color on the top of a bird's head, usually on the feathers of the forehead and crown.

CARPAL JOINT The bend of the wing, at the "wrist."

CHICK A young bird before it is able to fly.

CLUTCH A set of eggs laid and incubated together in the nest; if these are lost, a replacement clutch may be laid; some species have several clutches during the course of one breeding season, others ("single brooded") have only one.

COLONY A group of nests close together, often on the ground (e.g., gulls and terns) or in trees (e.g., herons).

COLOR RING OR BAND A plastic or metal band placed on a bird's leg; a combination of colors or numbers on the band allow individual recognition without having to capture the bird.

CORVID A bird of the crow family or corvidae.

COURTSHIP Usually ritualized behavior, male and female together forming a pair bond before breeding.

CRYPTIC Describes coloration that gives a bird camouflage or makes it harder to see.

DAWN CHORUS The loud chorus of bird song heard in spring from just before dawn, especially in woodland.

DISPLAY A form of ritualized behavior with a specific function, for example in courtship, or in distracting potential predators.

DISTRIBUTION The geographical range of a species, often split into breeding range, wintering range, and areas in which it may be seen on migration.

DRAKE A male duck (females are then "ducks").

DRUMMING The sound made in spring by a woodpecker vibrating its bill against a branch; also made by a snipe diving through the air with outer tail feathers extended and vibrating.

DUSTING "Bathing" in loose, dry sand, dust, or soil to help remove parasites from feathers.

ECLIPSE A dull plumage worn by male ducks and geese in summer.

EXTINCT Describes a species no longer living anywhere on Earth; if a species has disappeared from a country or region, but is still found elsewhere, it is properly described as having been "extirpated" from that area.

FALL A sudden large arrival of migrant birds, especially when caused by bad weather on the coast.

FERAL Describes a bird or species that has escaped from captivity to live wild.

FIELD "In the field" means "in the wild" or out of doors (as opposed to being captive, or held "in the hand").

FIELD GUIDE An identification guide to birds as they are seen wild and free.

FIELD OF VIEW The extent of the area that can be seen through a telescope or binoculars at a given distance, expressed in degrees (angular field of view) or distance (linear field of view); higher magnification typically results in a smaller field of view.

FLEDGLING A young bird that has just learned to fly and has its first covering of feathers.

FLOCK A group of birds behaving in some sort of unison: tight flocks (e.g., starlings in flight) are obvious, but loose, feeding flocks of birds in woodland may be less so.

GAME BIRD Usually used to describe one of the pheasant, partridge, grouse, or quail families—other birds commonly shot for sport include ducks and geese ("waterfowl").

GENUS A category in classification above species, indicating close relationships. Appears as the first word in a two- or three-word scientific name (e.g., *homo* in *homo sapiens*, or *falco* in *falco peregrinus*). Plural is "genera."

GORGET Band of color or pattern, such as streaks, around the bird's upper breast.

HABITAT The environment that a species requires for survival. Its characteristics include shelter, water, food, feeding areas, nest sites, and roosting sites. More loosely described in such terms as "lowland heath" or "deciduous woodland"; also used for particular times of year or types of behavior, e.g., muddy estuary, open sea, ploughed fields.

HEN A female bird.

IMMATURE Describes a bird not yet old enough to breed or have full adult plumage colors.

INCUBATION Maintenance of proper temperature of the egg to allow development of the embryo.

JIZZ A kind of indefinable quality that gives a species a character of its own, combining shape, color, and—especially—actions.

JUVENILE The young bird in its first full plumage. Also known as juvenal in the U.S.

LOAFING Sitting or standing, often in groups, apparently doing little or nothing. Gulls, for example, "loaf" for hours at a time.

MANDIBLE The jaw and its horny sheath; upper and lower mandibles together form the beak or bill.

MEASUREMENTS The size of a bird is usually indicated by the length from bill tip to tail tip on a bird laid out on a flat surface. In reality, the apparent "size" depends as much on shape and bulk as on simple length.

MIGRATION A regular, seasonal movement of birds from one region or continent to another, between alternate areas occupied at different times of year.

MOLT The replacement of a bird's feathers, in a regular sequence characteristic of each species. There may be a complete molt or a partial molt depending on the season.

NEST A receptacle built to take a clutch of eggs and, in many species, the young birds before they are able to fly; eggs may also be laid on a bare ledge or on the ground, with no nest structure being made.

NOCTURNAL Active at night.

NUMBERS Bird populations vary hugely from season to season, so are best described in terms of a particular measure that is easily repeated, usually "breeding pairs." In the case of large, more easily counted birds, such as ducks and geese, the measure is the total number of individuals at a certain season.

ORNITHOLOGY The study of birds: usually refers to scientific study of biology and ecology, while the hobby of watching birds is known simply as bird-watching or birding.

PASSAGE MIGRANT A species or bird seen in some intermediate area during its migration from summer to winter quarters (or vice versa).

PASSERINE A "perching bird."

PLUMAGE A covering of feathers; also often used to describe the overall colors and patterns of the feathers, defining a bird's appearance according to age, sex, and season.

PREENING Care of the feathers, especially using the bill to "zip" the structures back into place.

RACE A recognizable geographical group, or subspecies, within a species. Often there is no obvious border between groups, which blend (in a "cline") from one extreme to another. There may be more distinctive differences between isolated areas, such as islands, in which case the decision whether there are races, or separate species, can be difficult.

RARITY An individual bird in an area where it is not normally seen, or is seen in only very small numbers. A species with a small world population is "rare."

ROOST To sleep; also the area where birds sleep.

SCAPULARS A bunch of feathers on the shoulder.

SEABIRD A species that comes to land to nest, but otherwise lives at sea and is not normally seen inland.

SOARING Flight, often at a high level, in which the wings are held almost still, using air currents for lift and propulsion.

SONG A vocalization with a specific purpose and usually distinctive for each species: in particular, advertising the presence of a bird on its territory.

SPECIES A group, or groups, of individuals that can produce fertile young. Different species rarely interbreed naturally; if they do so, infertile hybrid offspring are produced.

TERRITORY An area defended for exclusive use by an individual bird or a family. Both breeding and winter-feeding territories may be defended.

TWITCHER A bird-watcher temporarily engaged in "twitching" (hearing of the presence of an individual rare bird and traveling with the intention of seeing it). Not then, despite the media's frequent incorrect usage, a bird-watcher, but a particular kind of bird-watcher.

WADER A plover, sandpiper, curlew, or related species; in North America, usually called a "shorebird." Since some do not wade and some do not live on the shore, neither word is entirely satisfactory.

WATERFOWL Ducks, geese, and swans. Also known as wildfowl.

EPHEMERA

BIRD EGGS PRINT (1893): Print of bird eggs with bird species names from *The Avifauna of Laysan and the Neighboring Islands. Courtesy of Smithsonian Libraries.*

BIRDS IN FLIGHT DRAWING: Ink drawing by Girolamo Mazzola Bedoli from the Italian Renaissance. *Courtesy of National Gallery of Art.*

BIRDS PAINTING (1840): Oil on canvas painting by unknown American artist in 19th century. *Courtesy of National Gallery of Art.*

BLACKBOARD SKETCH (1909): An illustrative plate of birds from *Blackboard Sketching* by Frederick Whitney. The book was geared towards educators and taught the art techniques of drawing on blackboards. *Courtesy of Public Domain Image Archive.*

BLUE JAY FEATHER. *Stock photo ©Shutterstock.*

DUCK DECOY PAINTING (1937): Watercolor and graphite on paper painting by Max Fernekes. *Courtesy of National Gallery of Art.*

FORK-TAILED FLYCATCHER (1840): Audubon print of a Fork-tailed flycatcher, Gordonia Lasianthus. *Courtesy of New York Public Library.*

HANDBOOK OF BIRDS OF EASTERN NORTH AMERICA (1895): Cover print of an illustrated handbook. *Courtesy of New York Public Library.*

HUMMINGBIRD PHOTOGRAPH: Male Broad-billed hummingbird. *Stock photo ©Shutterstock.*

JOHN JAMES AUDUBON PORTRAIT (1861): Photo of John James Audubon taken by Mathew B. Brady. Audubon was a self-taught artist and ornithologist known for his Birds of America drawings. *Courtesy of Library of Congress.*

MEADOW LARK (1840): Audubon print of a Meadow Starling or Meadow Lark male and female and nest. *Courtesy of New York Public Library.*

PIGEON PHOTOGRAPHS (1908): Aerial photos from Julius Neubronner's camera strapped to a homing pigeon. *Courtesy of Wikipedia Commons.*

SHEET MUSIC (1900): Sheet music booklet of the song "When the Birds Go North Again." *Courtesy of New York Public Library.*

WHITE ALBATROSSES AND PETRELS PHOTOGRAPH (1893): Photo of white albatrosses and petrels on nests taken by a collector for the research book *The Avifauna of Laysan and the Neighboring Islands. Courtesy of Smithsonian Libraries.*

YOUNG FRIGATE BIRD PHOTOGRAPH (1893): Photo taken by a collector for the research book *The Avifauna of Laysan and the Neighboring Islands. Courtesy of Smithsonian Libraries.*